P9-CKS-348

the Secret

the POWER

Rhonda Byrne

SIMON &
SCHUSTER

London · New York · Sydney · Toronto

A CBS COMPANY

First published in Great Britain in 2010 by Simon & Schuster UK Ltd
A CBS COMPANY

Copyright © 2010 by Making Good LLC. THE POWER and The Power logo are
trademarks of Making Good LLC. THE SECRET and The Secret logo are registered
trademarks of TS Production Limited Liability Company, acting through its registered
branch, TS Ltd., Luxembourg Branch.

www.thesecret.tv

This book is copyright under the Berne Convention.
No reproduction without permission.
All rights reserved.

The right of Making Good LLC to be identified as the author of this work has been
asserted in accordance with sections 77 and 78 of the Copyright, Designs and Patents
Act, 1988.

3 5 7 9 10 8 6 4 2

Simon & Schuster UK Ltd
1st Floor
222 Gray's Inn Road
London
WC1X 8HB

www.simonandschuster.co.uk

Simon & Schuster Australia
Sydney

www.simonandschuster.com.au

The information contained in this book is intended to be educational and not for
diagnosis, prescription or treatment of any kind of health disorder whatsoever. This
information should not replace consultation with a competent health care professional.
The content of this book is intended to be used as an adjunct to a rational and
responsible health care programme prescribed by a health care practitioner. The author
and publisher are in no way liable for any misuse of the material.

A CIP catalogue copy for this book is available from the British Library.

ISBN: 978-0-85720-170-6
ISBN: 978-0-85720-171-3 (ebook)

Original artwork by Nic George for Making Good LLC
Book design by Making Good LLC and Gozer Media P/L (Australia)

Printed and bound in Italy by L.E.G.O SpA

"It is the cause of all perfection
of all things throughout the universe."

The Emerald Tablet (circa 3000 bc)

Dedicated to you

Contents

Foreword

September 9, 2004, is a day I will never forget. It seemed like any other morning when I woke, but it would become the greatest day of my life.

Like most other people, I had struggled and worked hard to survive all my life, dealing with difficulties and obstacles as best I could. But 2004 had been an especially tough year for me, and the challenging circumstances literally brought me to my knees on September 9. My relationships, health, career, and finances appeared to be in an irretrievable state. I could see no way out of the mounting difficulties that surrounded me. And then it happened!

My daughter handed me a one-hundred-year-old book[1], and during the ninety minutes it took me to read the book, my entire life changed. I understood how everything had happened in my life, and I immediately knew what to do to change every circumstance into what I wanted.

---

1 Wallace Wattles, *The Science of Getting Rich*. The book is available as a free download on The Secret website, www.thesecret.tv.

I had discovered a secret, a secret that had been passed on through centuries but had been known by very few people throughout history.

From that moment, the world I saw was not the same world. Everything I had believed about the way life worked was the very *opposite* of how it really was. I had lived decades believing that things in life just happen to us. But now, I could see the incredible truth.

I could also see that the majority of people did not know this secret, and so I set out to share it with the world. Against every imaginable obstacle I created the film *The Secret*, and it was released to the world in 2006. Later the same year I wrote the book *The Secret*, which enabled me to share more of what I had discovered.

When *The Secret* was released, it traveled at lightning speed and was passed from one person to another across the planet. Today tens of millions of people in every country in the world have changed their lives in the most incredible ways with its knowledge.

As people learned how to change their lives with *The Secret*, they shared thousands of amazing stories with me, and I received more insights into why people experience such difficulties in their lives. And with those insights came the knowledge of *The Power* – knowledge that can change lives instantly.

The Secret reveals the law of attraction – the most powerful law that governs our lives. *The Power* contains the essence of everything I have learned since *The Secret* was released in 2006. In *The Power* you will come to understand that all it takes is just one thing to change your relationships, money, health, happiness, career, and your entire life.

You don't need to have read *The Secret* for *The Power* to change your life, because everything you need to know is contained in *The Power*. If you have read *The Secret*, then this book will add immeasurably to what you already know.

There is so much for you to know. There is so much for you to understand about yourself and your life. And it is all good. In fact it is beyond good, it is phenomenal!

Acknowledgments

My deepest gratitude to the greatest human beings in history, who risked their lives to ensure the knowledge and truth of life was preserved for future generations.

For the creation of the book, *The Power*, I want to thank the following people for their invaluable assistance in making this book what it is: Skye Byrne for her phenomenal editing and, together with Jan Child, for their guidance, encouragement, expertise, and invaluable input; Josh Gold for his fastidious scientific and historical research; Shamus Hoare of Gozer Media and Nic George for the book design; and Nic George for his original artwork and graphics, and dedication in working to create a powerful and beautiful book that will touch every person's life who holds it in their hands.

My deepest thanks to my publishers at Simon & Schuster: Carolyn Reidy and Judith Curr for their faith and willingness to open their minds and hearts to new ways so that together we can bring joy to billions; my editor Leslie Meredith who made the editing process of *The Power* a complete joy; copy editors Peg Haller, Kimberly Goldstein, and Isolde Sauer;

and the rest of the team at Simon & Schuster – Dennis Eulau, Lisa Keim, Eileen Ahearn, Darlene DeLillo, Twisne Fan, Kitt Reckord, and Donna Loffredo – for their tireless ongoing work.

My love and thanks to my work colleagues and dear friends who make up The Secret team, for their courage to open their minds to all possibilities and overcome every challenge so that we can bring joy to the world: Paul Harrington, Jan Child, Donald Zyck, Andrea Keir, Glenda Bell, Mark O'Connor, Damian Corboy, Daniel Kerr, Tim Patterson, Hayley Byrne, Cameron Boyle, Kim Vernon, Chye Lee, Lori Sharapov, Skye Byrne, Josh Gold, Nic George, Laura Jensen and Peter Byrne.

My thanks to lawyers Michael Gardiner and Susan Seah of Gardiner Seah; my deepest thanks to lawyers Brad Brian and Luis Li at Munger Tolles, for their guidance and expertise, for being a living example of integrity and truth, and for bringing positivity into my life.

To my dearest friends who continually inspire me to greatness: Elaine Bate, Bridget Murphy, Paul Suding, Mark Weaver, Fred Naider, Dani Hahn, Bobby Webb, James Sinclair, George Vernon, Carmen Vasquez, Helmer Largaespada, and last but not least, Angel Martin Velayos, whose spiritual light and faith causes me to lift myself to new levels so that I can fulfill my dream of bringing joy to billions.

To my daughters Hayley and Skye, who are my greatest teachers, and who light up my life every single day with their presence, and to my sisters Pauline, Glenda, Jan, and Kaye, for their never-ending love and support through the good times and through the challenging times. The sudden death and loss of our father in 2004 led me to the discovery of The Secret; during the process of writing *The Power*, our mother – our best friend – passed away, leaving us to continue on without her and be the best that we can be, and to love unconditionally so that we can make a difference in the world. From the bottom of my heart, thank you Mum, for everything.

INTRODUCTION

You are meant to have an *amazing* life!

You are meant to have everything you love and desire. Your work is meant to be exciting, and you are meant to accomplish all the things you would love to accomplish. Your relationships with your family and friends are meant to be filled with happiness. You are meant to have all the money you need to live a full, wonderful life. You are meant to be living your dreams – all of them! If you want to travel, you are meant to travel. If you would love to start a business, you are meant to start a business. If you would love to learn to dance or learn how to sail a yacht or study Italian, you are meant to do those things. If you would love to be a musician, a scientist, a business owner, an inventor, a performer, a parent, or whatever it is you would love to be, you are *meant* to be it!

When you wake up each day, you should be filled with excitement because you *know* the day is going to be full of great things. You are meant to be laughing and full of joy. You are meant to feel strong and safe. You are meant to feel good about yourself and know you're invaluable. Of course there will be challenges in your life, and you are meant to have them too, because they help you to grow, but you are meant to know

how to overcome problems and challenges. You are meant
to be victorious! You are meant to be happy! You are meant
to have an *amazing* life!

You were not born to struggle. You were not born to live
a life where the moments of joy are few and far between.
You were not born to toil in your work five days a week, with
fleeting moments of happiness on weekends. You were not
born to live with limited energy, feeling exhausted at the end
of each day. You were not born to worry or be afraid. You were
not born to suffer. What would be the point of your life? You
are meant to experience life to its fullest and have everything
you want and, at the same time, be filled with joy, health,
vitality, excitement, and love, because that is an amazing life!

The life of your dreams, everything you would love to
be, do, or have, has always been closer to you than you knew,
because the power to *everything* you want is inside you!

*"There is a supreme power and ruling force which
pervades and rules the boundless universe. You are
a part of this power."*

Prentice Mulford (1834-1891)
NEW THOUGHT AUTHOR

In this book I want to show you the way to an amazing
life. You will discover something incredible about yourself,
your life, and the universe. Life is so much easier than you

think it is, and as you come to understand the way life works, and the power you have inside you, you will experience the magic of life in its fullness – and then you will have an amazing life!

Now let the magic of your life begin.

WHAT IS THE POWER?

"What this power is I cannot say; all I know is that it exists."

Alexander Graham Bell (1847-1922)

INVENTOR OF THE TELEPHONE

Life is simple. Your life is made up of only two kinds of things – positive things and negative things. Each area of your life, whether it's your health, money, relationships, work, or happiness, is either positive or negative to you. You have plenty of money or you lack money. You are brimming with health or you lack health. Your relationships are happy or difficult. Your work is exciting and successful or dissatisfying and unsuccessful. You are filled with happiness or you don't feel good a lot of the time. You have good years or bad years, good times or bad times, good days or bad days.

If you have more negative things than positive things in your life, then something is very wrong and you know it. You see other people who are happy and fulfilled and whose lives are full of great things, and something tells you that you deserve all that too. And you're right; you *do* deserve a life overflowing with good things.

Most people who have a great life don't realize exactly what it was that they did to get it. But they *did* do something. They used the power that is the cause of everything good in life...

Without exception, every person who has a great life used *love* to achieve it. The power to have all the positive and good things in life is *love*!

Love has been talked about and written about since the beginning of time, in every religion, and by every great thinker, philosopher, prophet, and leader. But many of us have not truly understood their wise words. Even though their teachings were specifically for people in their time, their one truth and message to the world is still the same today: *love*, because when you love you are using the greatest power in the universe.

The Force of Love

"Love is an element which though physically unseen is as real as air or water. It is an acting, living, moving force . . . it moves in waves and currents like those of the ocean."

Prentice Mulford (1834–1891)
NEW THOUGHT AUTHOR

The kind of love that the greatest thinkers and saviors of the world talked about is very different from what most people understand love to be. It is much more than loving your family, friends, and favorite things, because love is not just a feeling: love is a positive force. Love is not weak, feeble, or soft. Love is *the* positive force of life! Love is the cause of *everything* positive and good. There are not a hundred different positive forces in life; there is only one.

Nature's great powers, like gravity and electromagnetism, are invisible to our senses, but their power is indisputable. Likewise, the force of love is invisible to us, but its power is in fact far greater than any of nature's powers. The evidence of its power can be seen everywhere in the world: without love, there is no life.

Take a moment to think about it: What would the world be without love? First of all, you wouldn't even exist; without love you couldn't have been born. None of your family and friends would have been born either. In fact, there wouldn't be a single human being on the planet. If the force of love ceased today, the entire human race would decrease and eventually die out.

Every single invention, discovery, and human creation came from the love in a human heart. If it were not for the love of the Wright Brothers, we could not fly in an airplane. If it were not for the love of scientists, inventors, and discoverers, we would not have electricity, heating, or light; nor would we be able to drive a car or use a phone, appliance, or any of the technology that makes life easier and more comfortable. Without the love of architects and builders, there would be no homes, buildings, or cities. Without love, there would be no medicines, doctors, or emergency facilities. No teachers, schools, or education. There would be no books, no paintings, and no music, because all of these things are created from the positive force of love. Take a look around you right now. Whatever you see that is a human creation would not be there without love.

"Take away love and our earth is a tomb."

Robert Browning (1812-1889)

POET

Love Is the Force That Moves You

Everything you want to be, do, or have comes from love. Without love, you wouldn't move. There would be no positive force to propel you to get up in the morning, to work, play, dance, talk, learn, listen to music, or do anything at all. You'd be like a stone statue. It is the positive force of love that inspires you to move and gives you the desire to be, do, or have anything. The positive force of love can create anything good, increase the good things, and change anything negative in your life. You have the power over your health, your wealth, your career, your relationships, and every area of your life. And that power – love – is inside you!

But if you have the power over your life, and that power is inside you, why isn't your life amazing? Why isn't every area of your life magnificent? Why don't you have everything you want? Why haven't you been able to do everything you want to do? Why aren't you filled with joy every day?

The answer is: because you have a choice. You have a choice whether to love and harness the positive force – or not. And whether you realize it or not, every day of your life

– every *moment* of your life – you have been making this choice. Without exception, every single time you experienced something good in your life, you loved and harnessed love's positive force. And every single time you experienced something not good, you didn't love, and the result was negativity. Love is the cause of all the good things in your life, and a lack of love is the cause of all the negative things and all the pain and suffering. Tragically, a lack of knowledge and understanding of the power of love is clear in people's lives across the planet today – and in the entire history of humanity.

> *"Love is the most powerful and still most unknown energy in the world."*
>
> Pierre Teilhard de Chardin (1881-1955)
> PRIEST AND PHILOSOPHER

Now, you are receiving the knowledge of the one and only power to all the good things in life, and you will be able to use it to change your entire life. But first, you must understand *exactly* how love works.

The Law of Love

The universe is governed by natural laws. We can fly in an airplane because aviation works in harmony with natural laws. The laws of physics didn't change for us to be able to fly, but we found a way to work in accordance with the natural laws, and by doing so we can fly. Just as laws of physics govern aviation, electricity, and gravity, there is a law that governs love. To harness the positive force of love and change your life, you must understand its law, the most powerful law in the universe – the law of attraction.

From the greatest to the smallest – the law of attraction is what holds every star in the universe and forms every atom and molecule. The force of attraction of the sun holds the planets in our solar system, keeping them from hurtling into space. The force of attraction in gravity holds you and every person, animal, plant, and mineral on earth. The force of attraction can be seen in all of nature from a flower attracting bees or a seed attracting nutrients from the soil, to every living creature being attracted to its own species. The force of attraction operates through all the animals on the earth, fish in the sea, and birds in the sky, leading them to multiply and form herds, schools, and flocks. The force of attraction holds together the cells of your body, the materials of your house, and the furniture you sit on, and it holds your car to the road and the water in your glass. Every object you use is held together by the force of attraction.

Attraction is the force that draws people to other people. It draws people to form cities and nations, groups, clubs, and societies where they share common interests. It is the force that pulls one person to science and another to cooking; it pulls people to various sports or to different styles of music, to certain animals and pets. Attraction is the force that draws you to your favorite things and places, and it's the force that draws you to your friends and the people you love.

The Attractive Force of Love

So what is the force of attraction? The force of attraction is the force of love! Attraction *is* love. When you feel an attraction to your favorite food, you're feeling love for that food; without attraction, you wouldn't feel anything. All food would be the same to you. You wouldn't know what you love or what you don't love, because you wouldn't be attracted to anything. You wouldn't be attracted to another person, a particular city, house, car, sport, job, music, clothes, or anything, because it's through the force of attraction that you feel love!

"The law of attraction or the law of love . . . they are one and the same."

Charles Haanel (1866-1949)
NEW THOUGHT AUTHOR

The law of attraction *is* the law of love, and it is the all-powerful law that keeps everything in harmony, from countless galaxies to atoms. It is operating in everything and through everything in the universe. And it is the law that is operating in your life.

In universal terms, the law of attraction says: like attracts like. What that means in simple terms for your life is: what you *give* out, you *receive* back. Whatever you give out in life is what you receive back in life. Whatever you give, by the law of attraction, is exactly what you attract back to yourself.

"To every action there is an equal and opposite reaction."

Isaac Newton (1643-1727)

MATHEMATICIAN AND PHYSICIST

GIVE   RECEIVE

Every action of *giving* creates an opposite action of *receiving* and what you receive is always equal to what you've given. Whatever you give out in life, must return to you. It is the physics and the mathematics of the universe.

Give positivity, you *receive* back positivity; *give* negativity, you *receive* back negativity. Give positivity and you receive back a life full of positive things. Give negativity and you receive back a life filled with negative things. And how do you give positivity or negativity? Through your thoughts and your feelings!

In any moment, you're giving either positive thoughts or negative thoughts. You're giving either positive feelings or negative feelings. And whether they're positive or negative will determine what you receive back in your life. All the people, circumstances, and events that make up every moment of your life are being attracted back to you through the thoughts and feelings you're giving out. Life doesn't just happen to you; you *receive* everything in your life based on what you've *given*.

> *"Give, and it will be given to you... for by your standard of measure it will be measured to you in return."*
>
> *Jesus* (CIRCA 5 BC–CIRCA AD 30)
> FOUNDER OF CHRISTIANITY, IN LUKE 6:38

What you give – you receive. Give help and support to a friend when he's moving house, and most surely that help and support will return to you with lightning speed.

Give anger to a family member who let you down, and that anger will also return to you, clothed in the circumstances of your life.

You are creating your life with your thoughts and your feelings. Whatever you think and feel creates everything that happens to you and everything you experience in your life. If you think and feel, "I've got a difficult and stressful day today," then you will attract back to you all people, circumstances, and events that will make your day difficult and stressful.

If you think and feel, "Life is really good to me," you will attract back to you all people, circumstances, and events that will make life really good for you.

You Are a Magnet

The law of attraction is unfailingly giving you every single thing in your life based on what you're giving out. You magnetize and receive the circumstances of wealth, health, relationships, your job, and every single event and experience in your life, based on the thoughts and feelings you're giving out. Give out positive thoughts and feelings about money, and you magnetize positive circumstances, people, and events that bring more money to you. Give out negative thoughts and feelings about money, and you magnetize negative circumstances, people, and events that cause you to have a lack of money.

"Whether humanity will consciously follow the law of love, I do not know. But that need not disturb me. The law will work just as the law of gravitation works whether we accept it or not."

Mahatma Gandhi (1869-1948)

<small>INDIAN POLITICAL LEADER</small>

As surely as you think and feel, the law of attraction is responding to you. It doesn't matter whether your thoughts and feelings are good or bad, you are giving them out, and they will return to you as automatically and precisely as an echo returns the same words you send out. But this means that you can change your life by changing your thoughts and feelings. Give positive thoughts and feelings, and you will change your entire life!

Positive and Negative Thoughts

Your thoughts are both the words you hear in your head and the words you speak out loud. When you say to somebody, "What a beautiful day," you had the thought first and then spoke the words. Your thoughts also become your actions. When you get out of bed in the morning, you had the thought of getting out of bed before you took action. You can't take any action without thinking the thought first.

It's your thoughts that determine whether your words and actions will be positive or negative. But how do you know whether your thoughts are positive or negative? Your thoughts are positive when they are thoughts of what you want and love! And negative thoughts are thoughts of what you don't want and don't love. It is that simple and that easy.

Whatever you want in your life, you want it because you love it. Take a moment and think about it. You don't want things you don't love, do you? Every person only wants what they love; nobody wants what they don't love.

When you think or talk about the things you want and love, such as, "I love those shoes, they're beautiful," your thoughts are positive, and those positive thoughts will come back to you as the things you love – beautiful shoes. When you think or talk about the things you don't want and don't love, such as "Look at the price of those shoes, that's highway robbery," your thoughts are negative, and those negative thoughts will come back to you as the things you don't love – things that are too expensive for you.

Most people think and talk about what they don't love *more* than they think and talk about what they love. They give out more negativity than love, and in doing so they are inadvertently depriving themselves of all the good things in life.

It's impossible to have a great life without love. People who have great lives think and talk about what they love *more* than what they don't love! And people who are struggling think and talk about what they don't love *more* than what they do love!

> *"One word frees us of all the weight and pain of life.*
> *That word is love."*
>
> *Sophocles* (496-406 BC)
> GREEK PLAYWRIGHT

Talk About What You Love

When you talk about any difficulties with money, a relationship, an illness, or even that the profits of your business are down, you are not talking about what you love. When you talk about a bad event in the news, or a person or situation that annoyed or frustrated you, you are not talking about what you love. Talking about the bad day you had, being late for an appointment, getting caught in traffic, or missing the bus are all talking about what you don't love. There are many little things that happen each day; if you get caught up in talking about what you don't love, every one of those little things brings more struggle and difficulty to your life.

You have to talk about the good news of the day. Talk about the appointment that went well. Talk about how you love being on time. Talk about how good it is to be full of health. Talk about the profits you want your business to achieve. Talk about the situations and interactions you had in your day that went well. You have to talk about what you love, to bring what you love to you.

If you parrot negative things and squawk about the things you don't love, you are literally jailing yourself, like a parrot in a cage. Every time you talk about what you don't love, you are adding another bar to the cage and you are locking yourself away from all the good.

People who have great lives talk *more* about what they love. By doing so, they gain unlimited access to all the good in life, and they are as free as the birds that soar in the sky. To have a great life, break the bars of the cage that is jailing you; give love, talk only about what you love, and love will set you free!

"Then you will know the truth and the truth will set you free."

Jesus (CIRCA 5 BC-CIRCA AD 30)

FOUNDER OF CHRISTIANITY, IN JOHN 8:32

Nothing is impossible for the force of love. No matter who you are, no matter what situation you may be facing, the force of love can set you free.

I know of a woman who through love alone broke the bars that caged her. She had been left in poverty and faced with bringing up her children by herself after twenty years of an abusive marriage. Despite the extreme hardship she faced, this woman never allowed resentment, anger, or any ill feeling to take root inside her. She never talked negatively about her ex-husband but instead gave only positive thoughts and words about her dream of a new, perfect, beautiful husband, and her dream of traveling to Europe. Even though she had no money to travel, she applied for and got a passport and bought small items she would need on her dream trip to Europe.

Well, she did meet her perfect and beautiful new husband. And after marrying, they moved to her husband's home in Spain overlooking the ocean, where she now lives in happiness.

This woman refused to talk about what she didn't love but instead chose to give love and think and talk about what she loved, and in doing so, she set herself free from hardship and suffering, and received a beautiful life.

You can change your life, because you have an unlimited ability to think and talk about what you love, and so you have an unlimited ability to bring everything good in life to you! However, the power you have is far greater than giving positive thoughts and words of the things you love, because the law of attraction is responding to your thoughts *and* your feelings. You have to *feel* love to harness its power!

"Love is the fulfilling of the law."

Saint Paul (CIRCA 5-67)

CHRISTIAN APOSTLE, IN ROMANS 13:10

POINTS OF POWER

- *Love is not weak, feeble, or soft. Love is the positive force of life! Love is the cause of everything positive and good.*

- *Everything you want to be, do, or have comes from love.*

- *The positive force of love can create anything good, increase the good things, and change anything negative in your life.*

- *Every day, in every moment, you make the choice whether to love and harness the positive force – or not.*

- *The law of attraction is the law of love, and it is the law that is operating in your life.*

- *Whatever you give out in life is what you receive back in life. Give positivity, you receive back positivity; give negativity, you receive back negativity.*

- *Life doesn't happen to you; you receive everything in your life based on what you've given.*

- *Whether your thoughts and feelings are good or bad, they return as automatically and precisely as an echo.*

- *People who have great lives think and talk about what they love more than what they don't love!*

- *Talk about the good news of the day. Talk about what you love. And bring what you love to you.*

- *You have an unlimited ability to think and talk about what you love, and so you have an unlimited ability to bring everything good in life to you!*

- *Love, because when you love you are using the greatest power in the universe.*

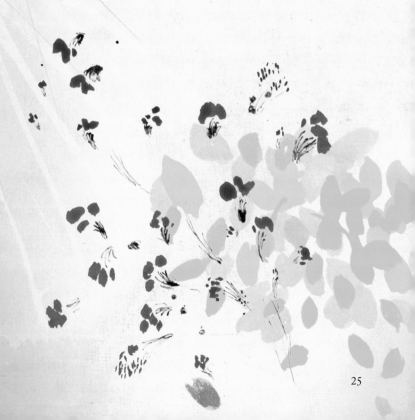

THE POWER
OF FEELINGS

"Feeling is the secret."

Neville Goddard (1905-1972)

<small>New Thought author</small>

You're a Feeling Being

From the moment you are born, you are always feeling something, and so is every other person. You can stop your conscious thoughts when you're sleeping, but you can never stop feeling, because to be alive is to feel life. You are a feeling "being" to the core of you, and so it's no accident that every part of your human body is created so you can feel life!

You have the sense of sight, hearing, taste, smell, and touch, so that you can feel everything in life. They are "feeling" senses, because they enable you to feel what you see, feel what you hear, feel what you taste, feel what you smell and touch. Your entire body is covered with a fine layer of skin, which is a feeling organ, so you can *feel* everything.

How you feel in any one moment is more important than anything else, because how you feel right now is creating your life.

Your Feelings Are the Fuel

Your thoughts and words have no power at all in your life without your feelings. You think so many thoughts in a day that don't amount to anything because many of your thoughts don't elicit a strong feeling within you. It's what you *feel* that matters!

Imagine your thoughts and words as being like a rocket ship, and your feelings as the fuel. A rocket ship is a stationary vehicle that can't do anything without fuel, because the fuel is the power that lifts the rocket ship. It's the same with your thoughts and words. Your thoughts and words are vehicles that can't do anything without your feelings, because your feelings are the power of your thoughts and words!

If you think, "I can't stand my boss," that thought is expressing a strong negative *feeling* you have about your boss, and you're giving out that negative *feeling*. As a consequence, your relationship with your boss will continue to get worse.

If you think, "I work with some fabulous people in my job," those words are expressing the positive *feeling* you have about the people you work with and you're giving out that positive *feeling*. As a consequence, your relationships with your work colleagues will continue to get better.

> *"The emotions must be called upon to give feeling to the thought so it will take form."*
>
> *Charles Haanel* (1866-1949)
>
> NEW THOUGHT AUTHOR

Good and Bad Feelings

Like everything else in life, your feelings can be either positive or negative; you have good feelings or bad feelings. All good feelings come from love! And all negative feelings come from a lack of love. The better you feel, like when you feel joyful, the more love you give out. And the more love you *give*, the more you *receive*.

The worse you feel, like when you feel despair, the more negativity you give out. And the more negativity you give, the more negativity you receive back in life. The reason you feel so bad with negative feelings is because *love* is the positive force of life, and negative feelings don't have much love in them!

The better you feel, the better life gets.

The worse you feel, the worse life gets – until you change how you feel.

When you feel good, your thoughts are automatically good too. You cannot feel good and have negative thoughts at the same time! Likewise it's impossible for you to feel bad and have good thoughts at the same time.

How you feel is an exact reflection, a precise measure to the finest degree, of what you are giving out in any moment. When you feel good, you don't have to be concerned about anything else because your thoughts, words, and actions will be good. Simply by feeling good you are guaranteed to be giving love, and all of that love must come back to you!

Good Means Good

Most people understand how it feels to feel good or really bad but don't realize they are living with negative feelings a lot of the time. People think that feeling bad means feeling extreme negativity, such as sadness, grief, anger, or fear, and while feeling bad does include all those feelings, negative feelings come in many degrees.

If you feel "okay" most of the time, you may think that feeling "okay" is a positive feeling because you don't feel really bad. If you've been feeling really bad and you now feel okay then most certainly feeling okay is far better than feeling really bad. But feeling okay most of the time is a negative feeling, because feeling okay is not feeling good. Feeling good means feeling good! Good feelings mean you're happy, joyful, excited, enthusiastic, or passionate. When you're feeling okay, average, or you're not really feeling anything much at all, then your life will be okay, average, or not much at all! That is not a good life. Good feelings mean you feel really good, and feeling really good is what brings a really good life!

"The measure of love is love without measure."

Saint Bernard of Clairvaux (1090-1153)

CHRISTIAN MONK AND MYSTIC

When you're feeling joyful, you are giving joy, and you'll receive back joyful experiences, joyful situations, and joyful people, wherever you go. From the smallest experience of your favorite song playing on the radio to bigger experiences of receiving a pay raise – all of the circumstances you experience are the law of attraction responding to your feeling of joy. When you're feeling irritated, you're giving irritation, and you'll receive back irritating experiences, irritating situations, and irritating people wherever you go. From the small irritation of a mosquito, to the bigger irritation of your car breaking down, all of these experiences are the law of attraction responding to your irritation.

Every good feeling unites you with the force of love, because love is the source of all good feelings. Feelings of enthusiasm, excitement, and passion come from love, and when you feel any of them consistently, they give you a life filled with enthusiastic, exciting, and passionate things.

You can harness the power of a good feeling to the fullest by turning up its volume. To turn up the volume of a feeling, take charge of it and deliberately intensify it so you feel as good as you can. To amplify enthusiasm, revel in the feeling of enthusiasm; milk the feeling for all that you can by feeling it intensely! When you feel passion or excitement, revel in those feelings and intensify them by feeling them as deeply as you can. The more you amplify your good feelings, the greater the love you give, and the results you will receive back in your life will be nothing short of spectacular.

When you're feeling any good feeling, you can also amplify it by looking for things you love. Before sitting down to write this book, each day I spent several minutes amplifying my good feelings. To amplify my good feelings, I thought about all the things I love. I counted the things I love nonstop one after the other: my family, friends, home, flowers in the garden, the weather, colors, situations, events, and things I loved that happened during the week, month, or year. I kept listing everything I love in my mind until I felt amazing. Then I sat down to write. It's as easy as that to amplify your good feelings, and you can do it anywhere, at any time.

Your Feelings Reflect What You're Giving

You can tell right now in the major areas of your life whether you have been giving more good feelings or more bad feelings. How you *feel* about each subject in your life, such as money, health, your job, and every individual relationship, is an exact reflection of what you have been giving out on each subject.

When you think about money, your feelings reflect what you are giving about money. If you feel bad when you think about money, because you don't have enough, you must receive back negative circumstances and experiences of not having enough money – because that is the negative feeling you're giving.

When you think about your job, your feelings tell you what you are giving about your job. If you feel good about your job, you must receive back positive circumstances and experiences in your job – because that is the positive feeling you're giving. When you think about your family, health, or any subject that is important to you, your feelings tell you what you're giving.

"Be careful of your moods and feelings, for there is an unbroken connection between your feelings and your visible world."

Neville Goddard (1905-1972)
NEW THOUGHT AUTHOR

Life isn't happening to you; life is *responding* to you. Life is your call! Every area of your life is your call. You are the creator of your life. You are the writer of your life story. You are the director of your life movie. You decide what your life will be – by what you give out.

There are infinite levels of good feelings you can feel, which means there's no end to the heights of the life you can receive. There are also many levels of bad feelings that become increasingly negative, but with bad feelings there is a bottom limit beyond which you can't endure, which forces you to choose good feelings again.

It's not a fluke or an accident that good feelings feel amazing and that bad feelings feel really bad. Love is the supreme ruling power of life, and it calls you and attracts you through your good feelings, so you will live the life you are meant to live. Love also calls you through your bad feelings, because they tell you that you are disconnected from the positive force of life!

Everything Is About How You Feel

Everything in life is about how you feel. Every decision you make in your life is based on how you feel. The single motivating power of your entire life is your feelings!

Whatever you want in your life, you want it because you love it and because it will make you *feel* good. Whatever you don't want in your life you don't want because it will make you *feel* bad.

You want health because it feels good to be healthy, and it feels bad to be sick. You want money because it feels good to buy and do the things you love, and it feels bad when you can't. You want happy relationships because they make you feel good, and difficult relationships make you feel bad. You want happiness because happiness feels good, and to be unhappy feels bad.

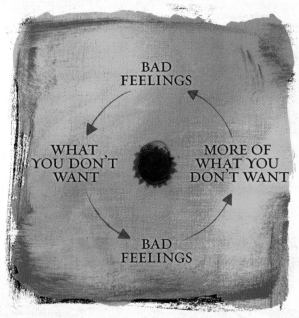

All the things you want are motivated by the good feelings they will give you! And how do you receive the good things you want in your life? Good feelings! Dollars want you. Health wants you. Happiness wants you. All the things you love want you! They are bursting to come into your life, but you have to give good feelings to bring them to you. You don't have to battle and struggle to change the circumstances of your life; all you have to do is give love through good feelings, and what you want will appear!

Your good feelings harness the force of love – the power to everything good in life. Your good feelings tell you this is the way to what you want. Your good feelings tell you that when you feel good, life will be good! But you have to give good feelings first!

If you have been living your life saying to yourself, "I will be happy when I have a better house," "I will be happy when I get a job or promotion," "I will be happy when the kids are through college," "I will be happy when we have more money," "I will be happy when I can travel," or "I will be happy when my business is a success," you will never have those things because your thoughts are defying the way love works. They're defying the law of attraction.

You have to be happy first, and *give* happiness, to *receive* happy things! It can't happen any other way, because whatever you want to *receive* in life, you must *give* first! You are in command of your feelings, you are in command of your love, and the force of love will give back to you whatever you give out.

POINTS OF POWER

- *How you feel in any one moment is more important than anything else, because how you feel right now is creating your life.*

- *Your feelings are the power of your thoughts and words. It's what you feel that matters!*

- *All good feelings come from love! All negative feelings come from a lack of love.*

- *Every good feeling unites you with the force of love, because love is the source of all good feelings.*

- *Amplify your good feelings by thinking about all the things you love. Count the things you love nonstop one after the other. Keep listing everything you love until you feel amazing.*

- *How you feel about each subject in your life is an exact reflection of what you have been giving out on each subject.*

- *Life isn't happening to you – life is responding to you! Every subject of your life is your call and you make the call on everything in life by what you give.*

- *There are infinite levels of good feelings you can feel, which means there is no end to the heights of life you can receive.*

- *All the things you love want you! Dollars want you. Health wants you. Happiness wants you.*

- *Don't struggle to change the circumstances of your life. Give love through your good feelings and what you want will appear!*

- *You have to give good feelings first. You have to be happy first, and give happiness, to receive happy things! Whatever you want to receive in life, you must give first!*

FEELING
FREQUENCIES

If You Can Feel It, You Can Receive It

Everything in the universe is magnetic and everything has a magnetic frequency. Your feelings and thoughts have magnetic frequencies too. Good feelings mean you're on a positive frequency of love. Bad feelings mean you're on a negative frequency. Whatever you feel, whether good or bad, determines your frequency, and like a magnet you attract the people, events, and circumstances that are on the same frequency!

If you are feeling enthusiastic, your frequency of enthusiasm will attract enthusiastic people, situations, and events. If you are feeling fearful, your frequency of fear will attract fearful people, situations, and events to you. You are never left in any doubt about the frequency you're on because your frequency is always exactly whatever you're feeling! You can change your frequency at any time by changing how you feel, and everything around you will change because you're on a new frequency.

You can take any situation in your life, and every possible outcome of that situation can happen. Any outcome can happen because you can have any feeling about the situation!

A relationship can be on a happy, joyful, exciting, satisfying, and every good feeling frequency. A relationship can also be on a boring, frustrating, worrisome, resentful, depressing, and every bad feeling frequency. Any outcome of that relationship can happen! And the way you feel determines exactly what will happen in that relationship. Whatever feeling you are giving about the relationship is exactly what you will receive back in the relationship. If you're feeling joyful about the relationship most of the time, you're giving love, and you must receive love and joy back through that relationship because that's the frequency you're on.

> *"A change of feeling is a change of destiny."*
>
> *Neville Goddard* (1905-1972)
> NEW THOUGHT AUTHOR

Look at the list of feeling frequencies and you'll see that no matter what the subject in your life, there are many different feeling frequencies. And you determine the outcome of each subject through how you feel about it!

You can feel excited, happy, joyful, hopeful, worried, fearful, or depressed about money. You can feel ecstatic, passionate, blissful, discouraged, or anxious about your health.

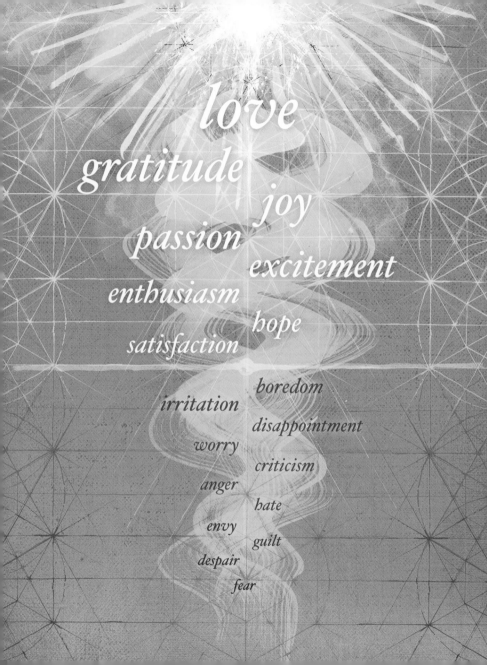

These are all different feeling frequencies, and whatever feeling frequency you're on is what you will receive.

You may want to travel, but if you feel disappointment that you don't have the money to travel, then on the subject of travel, you are feeling disappointment. Feeling disappointment means you're on the disappointment frequency, and you will continue to receive disappointing circumstances in which you cannot travel, until you change the way you feel. The force of love will move every circumstance for you to travel, but you have to be on one of the good feeling frequencies to receive it.

When you change the way you feel about a situation, you are giving a different feeling, you're on a different feeling frequency, and the situation *must* change to mirror your new frequency. If something negative has happened in your life, you can change it. It is never too late, because you can always change the way you feel. To receive what you would love, to change anything into what you would love, no matter what the subject, *all* it takes is changing the way you feel!

"If you want to find the secrets of the Universe, think in terms of energy, frequency, and vibration."

Nikola Tesla (1856-1943)

INVENTOR OF THE RADIO AND ALTERNATING CURRENT

Take Your Feelings Off Automatic Pilot

Many people don't know about the power of good feelings, and so their feelings are reactions or responses to what happens to them. They have put their feelings on automatic pilot, instead of deliberately taking charge of them. When something good happens, they feel good. When something bad happens, they feel bad. They don't realize that their feelings are the *cause* of what is happening to them. As they react with negative feelings to something that has happened, they *give* out more negative feelings, and they *receive* back more negative circumstances. They become trapped in a cycle by their own feelings. Their life goes around and around in circles not getting anywhere, like a hamster on a wheel, because they don't realize that to change their life, they must change their feeling frequency!

> *"It's not what happens to you, but how you react to it that matters."*
>
> *Epictetus* (55-135)
> GREEK PHILOSOPHER

If you don't have enough money, naturally you don't feel good about money, but the money in your life will never change while you don't feel good about it. If you give out negative feelings about money, you're on a negative frequency about money and you will receive back negative circumstances such as big bills or things breaking down, which are all circumstances that drain you of money. When you react with negative feelings to a big bill, you give out more negative feelings about money, which bring even more negative circumstances to you that drain you of more money.

Every single second is an opportunity to change your life, because in any moment you can change the way you feel. It doesn't matter what you have felt before. It doesn't matter what mistakes you think you may have made. When you change the way you feel, you are on a different frequency, and the law of attraction responds instantaneously! When you change the way you feel, the past has gone! When you change the way you feel, your life changes.

"Do not waste one moment in regret, for to think feelingly of the mistakes of the past is to re-infect yourself."

Neville Goddard (1905-1972)
NEW THOUGHT AUTHOR

No Excuses for the Force of Love

If your life is not filled with everything you love, it doesn't mean you're not a good and loving person. The life purpose for each of us is to overcome negativity by choosing love. The problem is that most people love and then stop loving hundreds of times in a day. They don't give love long enough for the force of love to move all the good things into their life. Think about it: one moment you give love through a warm hug with a loved one, and then you stop giving love within minutes when you get annoyed because you can't find your keys or you're delayed in traffic or you can't find a parking space. You give love when you laugh with a work colleague, and then stop when you get disappointed because the local lunch place has run out of something you want. You give love as you look forward to the weekend, and then you stop when you receive your bills. And so it continues all through the day; you give love and you stop giving love, give love and stop giving love, give love and stop giving love, from one moment to the next.

You are either giving love and harnessing the force of love, or you're not. You can't harness the force of love with an excuse about why you didn't love. Excuses and justifying why you didn't love just add more negativity to your life. When you give an excuse as to why you didn't love, you're feeling the same negativity again, and so you're giving out more of it!

"Holding on to anger is like grasping a hot coal with the intent of throwing it at someone else; you are the one getting burned."

Gautama Buddha (563–483 BC)

FOUNDER OF BUDDHISM

If you get annoyed because there was a mix-up in an appointment, and you blame the other person for the mix-up, you are using blame as your excuse not to give love. But the law of attraction only receives what *you* are giving, so if you're giving blame, you must receive circumstances of blame back in your life. It won't necessarily come back to you from the person you were blaming, but most assuredly you will receive a circumstance of blame. There are no excuses for the force of love. You get what you give – period.

Every Little Thing Is Included

Blame, criticism, finding fault, and complaining are all forms of negativity. All of them bring so much strife. With every little complaint and every moment you criticize anything, you are giving negativity. Complaints about the weather, traffic, the government, your partner, children, parents, long lines, the economy, food, your body, your work, customers, businesses, prices, noise, or service seem like small harmless things, but they bring back with them a whole host of negativity.

Throw out of your vocabulary words like *terrible*, *horrible*, *disgusting*, and *awful*, because when you say those words, they come with strong feelings. When you say them they must return to you, which means you are putting those labels on your life! Don't you think it would be a good idea to use more words like *fantastic*, *amazing*, *fabulous*, *brilliant*, and *wonderful?*

You can have whatever you love and want, but you have to harmonize with love, and that means there are no excuses for not giving love. Excuses and justifications prevent you from receiving everything you want. They prevent you from having an amazing life.

> *"All that we send into the lives of others comes back into our own."*
>
> *Edwin Markham* (1852-1940)
>
> POET

You don't make a connection when you complain to a store person and then a few hours later you receive a call from your neighbor complaining that your dog is barking. You don't make a connection when you meet a friend for lunch and talk negatively about a mutual friend and you arrive back at work to discover big problems have developed with your major client. You don't make a connection when your dinner conversation is about something negative in the news and that night you can't sleep because of an upset stomach.

You don't make a connection when you stop to help someone who has dropped something in the street and ten minutes later you get a parking space right outside the supermarket door. You don't make a connection when you happily help your child with their homework and the next day you receive news that your tax refund will be bigger than you thought. You don't make a connection when you do a favor for a friend and, that same week, your boss gives you two complimentary tickets to a sports game. In every circumstance and moment of your life you are receiving what you have given, whether you make the connection or not.

> *"Nothing comes from without. All things come from within."*
>
> *Neville Goddard* (1905-1972)
> NEW THOUGHT AUTHOR

The Tipping Point

If you give more than 50 percent positive thoughts and feelings instead of negative, you have reached a tipping point. Even if you just give 51 percent good thoughts and good feelings, you have tipped the scales of your life! And here's the reason why.

When you give love, it not only comes back to you as positive circumstances that you love, but as it comes back, it adds even *more* love and positivity to your life! The new positivity then attracts more positive things, adding even *more* love and positivity to your life, and so it continues. Everything is magnetic, and when something good comes to you, it magnetically attracts more good things.

You may have experienced this when you said you were having a "lucky streak" or you were "on a roll," when one good thing after another happened, and the good things just kept happening. The only reason those times occurred was because you had given out more love than negativity, and as the love returned to you, it added more love to your life, which then attracted even more good things.

You may have also experienced the reverse happening when something went wrong, and then other things started going wrong one after the other. Those times happened because you gave more negativity than love, and as the negativity returned to you, it added more negativity to your life, which then attracted even more negative things. You may have called those times "a run of bad luck," but they have nothing to do with luck at all. The law of attraction was working precisely in your life, and those times, good or bad, were simply a reflection of the percentage of love or negativity you were giving. The only reason the "lucky streak" or "run of bad luck" changed is that, at some point, you tipped the scales the other way with your feelings.

> *"It is thus that you may lead a charmed life and be forever protected from all harm; it is thus you may become a positive force whereby conditions of opulence and harmony may be attracted to you."*
>
> *Charles Haanel* (1866-1949)
> NEW THOUGHT AUTHOR

To change your life, all you have to do is tip the scales by giving 51 percent love through your good thoughts and good feelings. Once you reach the tipping point of giving more love than negativity, the love that comes back to you then multiplies itself by attracting more love through the law of attraction. Suddenly you experience an acceleration and multiplication of good things! Instead of more negative things coming back to you and multiplying, you now have more good things coming back to you and being multiplied in every area of your life. And this is the way your life is supposed to be.

When you wake up each morning, you are standing at the tipping point of your day. One way tips you into a wonderful day filled with good things, and the other way tips you into a day filled with problems. You are the one who determines what your day will be – by the way that you feel! Whatever you're feeling is what you're giving, and with certainty, that is exactly what you will receive back in your day, surrounding you wherever you go.

As you begin your day and you're feeling happy, while you keep feeling happy, your day will be great! But if you begin your day in a bad mood, and you do nothing to change it, your day will not be great at all.

One day of good feelings not only changes your day, it changes your tomorrow, and your life! Provided you maintain your good feelings and you go to sleep feeling good, you begin the next day with a momentum of good feelings. As you continue to feel good as much as you can, your good feelings continue to multiply by the law of attraction, and so it continues day after day, and your life gets better and better.

"Live today. Not yesterday. Not tomorrow. Just today. Inhabit your moments. Don't rent them out to tomorrow."

Jerry Spinelli (B. 1941)
CHILDREN'S AUTHOR

So many people don't live for today. They are completely consumed with the future, and yet it is how we live *today* that creates our future. It is what you feel *today* that matters, because it is the *only* thing that determines your future. Every day is an opportunity for a new life, because every single day you stand at the tipping point of your life. And on any one day you can change the future – through the way that you feel. When you tip the balance to good feelings, the force of love will change your life so fast that you will scarcely believe it.

POINTS OF POWER

- *Everything in the universe is magnetic and everything has a magnetic frequency, including your thoughts and feelings.*

- *Whatever you feel, whether good or bad, determines your frequency, and you attract the people, events, and circumstances that are on the same frequency.*

- *Change your frequency at any time by changing how you feel, and everything around you will change because you're on a new frequency.*

- *If something negative has happened in your life, you can change it. It is never too late, because you can always change the way you feel.*

- *Many people put their feelings on automatic pilot; their feelings are reactions to what happens to them. However, they don't realize that it's their feelings that are the cause of what happens to them.*

- *To change anything – whether it's the circumstances of money, health, relationships or any subject whatsoever – you have to change the way you feel!*

- *Blame, criticism, finding fault, and complaining are all forms of negativity, and all of them bring back nothing but strife.*

- *Throw out of your vocabulary words like terrible, horrible, disgusting, and awful. Use more words like fantastic, amazing, fabulous, brilliant, and wonderful.*

- *Even if you just give 51 percent good thoughts and good feelings, you have tipped the scales of your life!*

- *Every day is an opportunity for a new life. Every day you stand at the tipping point of your life. And on any one day you can change the future – through the way that you feel.*

THE POWER
AND CREATION

"Every moment of your life is infinitely creative and the Universe is endlessly bountiful. Just put forth a clear enough request, and everything your heart desires must come to you."

Shakti Gawain (B. 1948)

AUTHOR

In these next chapters you will learn how easy it is to harness the force of love for money, health, career, business, and relationships. With this knowledge, you will be able to change your life into whatever you want.

To bring a specific desire to you, follow the simple steps of the Creation Process. Whether it's bringing something you want or changing something you don't want, the process is always the same.

The Creation Process

Imagine it. Feel it. Receive it.

1. IMAGINE

Use your mind to focus on and imagine what you desire. Imagine yourself *being* with your desire. Imagine yourself *doing* things with your desire. Imagine yourself *having* your desire.

2. FEEL

At the same time as you imagine, you must *feel* love for what you're imagining. You must imagine and *feel* being with your desire. You must imagine and *feel* doing things with your desire. You must imagine and *feel* having your desire.

Your imagination connects you to what you want. Your desire and feelings of love create the magnetism, the magnetic power, drawing your desire to you. This completes your part in the Creation Process.

3. RECEIVE

The force of love will work through the visible and invisible forces of nature to bring what you desire to you. It will use circumstances, events, and people to give what you love to you.

Whatever you desire you must want it with all your heart. Desire *is* love, and unless you have a burning desire in your heart, you will not have enough power to harness the force of love. You must really desire what you want, as an athlete desires to play a sport, a dancer desires to dance, and a painter desires to paint. You must desire what you want with all your heart because desire is a feeling of love, and you must give love to receive what you love!

Whatever you want to be in your life, whatever you want to do in your life, whatever you want to have in your life, the Creation Process is the same. Give love to receive love. Imagine it. Feel it. Receive it.

When using the Creation Process, imagine and feel that you have what you want already, and never deviate from that state of being. Why? Because the law of attraction copies whatever you give, and so you must imagine and feel having it now!

If you want to lose weight, then give love by imagining and feeling yourself with the body you love, instead of imagining and feeling that you're overweight every single day. If you want to travel, then give love by imagining and feeling yourself traveling, instead of imagining every day that you don't have the money to travel. If you want to improve yourself in a sport, acting, singing, playing a musical instrument, hobby, or in your job, then give love for what you want to be by imagining and feeling whatever it is you would love to be. If you want a better marriage or a better relationship with anybody, then give love by imagining and feeling what it would be like to have that relationship.

"Faith is to believe that which you do not yet see; and the reward of this faith is to see that which you believe."

Saint Augustine of Hippo (354-430)

THEOLOGIAN AND BISHOP

When you begin working with the Creation Process, you might want to start by attracting something unusual. When you specifically attract something unusual, you will be left in no doubt about your power when you receive it.

One young woman began by choosing to attract a specific flower, a white calla lily. She imagined holding the flower in her hand, smelling the flower, and she felt having that calla lily. Two weeks later she went to a friend's house for dinner, and there in the centerpiece of the table was a bouquet of white calla lilies, the very flower and color she had imagined. She was excited to see the lilies, but she didn't say anything to her friend about her imagined flower. As she was walking out the door at the end of the evening, her friend's daughter spontaneously plucked one white calla lily from the vase and put it in her hand!

"Imagination is the beginning of creation.
You imagine what you desire, you will what you
imagine, and at last you create what you will."

George Bernard Shaw (1856-1950)
NOBEL PRIZE–WINNING PLAYWRIGHT

Give It – Receive It

Remember that the law of attraction says whatever you give, you receive. If you think of the law of attraction as a mirror, an echo, a boomerang, or a copying machine, it will help make you clearer on what to imagine and feel. The law of attraction is like a mirror because a mirror reflects back exactly what is in front of it. The law of attraction is like an echo because whatever you give out is exactly the echo that comes back. The law of attraction is like a boomerang, because whatever boomerang you throw is the exact same boomerang that comes back to you. The law of attraction is like a copying machine, because whatever you give is reproduced exactly and you will receive back an exact copy.

A few years ago I was in Paris for my work and I was walking down a street when a woman rushed past me wearing one of the most beautiful skirts I had seen, intricately detailed in a Parisian style. My reaction was love: "What a beautiful skirt!"

A few weeks later I was happily driving to work in Melbourne, Australia, when I was forced to stop because another driver was trying to do an illegal U-turn at an intersection. As I looked at a store window where I had been forced to stop, I saw the exact same skirt I had seen on the woman in the streets of Paris. I could not believe my eyes. When I got to work, I called the store and they told me they had received only one skirt from Europe in that style, and it was the skirt in the window. Of course the skirt was my size. When I went to the store to purchase the skirt, it was reduced to half price, and the store attendant told me they had not ordered the skirt, and that it had just appeared in their order accidentally!

The only thing I had done to bring that skirt to me was to love it, and from Paris to a suburban street in Australia, through circumstances and events, the exact same skirt was delivered to me. That is the magnetic power of love! That is love's law of attraction in operation.

Imagination

"This world is but a canvas to our imaginations."

Henry David Thoreau (1817-1862)

TRANSCENDENTALIST AUTHOR

When you imagine anything positive that you want and love, you are harnessing the force of love. When you imagine something positive, something good, and you feel love for it, that is what you are giving – and that is what you will receive. If you can imagine it and feel it, then you can receive it. But what you're imagining must come from love!

Whatever you're imagining must not harm another person. Imagining something that brings harm to another person comes not from love but from a lack of love. And with certainty any negativity, even imagined, will turn back with an equal ferocity on the person who sent it! Whatever you give, *you* receive back.

But I want to tell you something fantastic about the force of love and your imagination. The highest and best thing you think is possible is nothing compared to what the force of love can give to you. Love has no limits! If you want to be full of vitality and happiness, with an incredible zest for life, the force of love can give you health and happiness at levels far beyond what you have seen. I am telling you this so that you can start to break the boundaries of your imagination and stop putting limits on your life. Push your imagination to the limits, and imagine the best and highest that you possibly can of whatever it is that you want.

The difference between someone who is struggling and someone who has a fabulous life comes down to one thing – love. Those who have a great life imagine what they love

and want, and they *feel* the love of what they're imagining
more than other people! People who are struggling are
unintentionally using their imagination for what they don't
love and don't want, and are *feeling* the negativity of what
they're imagining. It's such a simple thing, but it creates vast
differences in people's lives, and you can see the difference
everywhere you look.

> *"The secret of the master mind is found wholly
> in the use of imagination."*
>
> *Christian D. Larson* (1874-1962)
> NEW THOUGHT AUTHOR

History has proven that those who dare to imagine the
impossible are the ones who break all human limitations.
In every field of human endeavor, whether science, medicine,
sports, the arts, or technology, the names of the people
who imagined the impossible are engraved in our history.
By breaking the limits of their imagination, they changed
the world.

Your entire life is what you have imagined it to be.
Everything you have or don't have, every situation and
circumstance of your life is what you have imagined it to be.
The problem is that many people imagine the worst! They're
turning the most wonderful tool against themselves. Instead of
imagining the best, many people are in fear and imagine all the
things that can go wrong. And as surely as they keep imagining

and feeling those things, they happen. Whatever you give, you receive. Feel and imagine the best and the highest you can in every area of your life, because the best you can imagine is a "piece of cake" for the force of love!

When my family had settled in the United States, we flew our fifteen-year-old dog, Cabbie, to be with us. One night, not long after Cabbie had arrived, he managed to get out of a small gap in the fence. Our home backs onto mountains, so it was far from an ideal situation. In the dark we searched the streets and the trails leading up to the mountains, but our dog was nowhere to be found.

As my daughter and I were searching, negative feelings of anguish began to increase. I knew we had to stop searching and change the way we were feeling inside immediately. The negative feelings were telling us that we were imagining the worst, and we had to change the way we were feeling quickly and imagine the best. At that point, every possible outcome could still happen, and we had to choose the outcome of having Cabbie safely home with us, by imagining and feeling that he was home.

We returned home and we pretended our dog was with us. We put food in his bowl as though he were there. We imagined hearing the bell around Cabbie's neck as he walked down our hallway. We talked to him and called out his name, as though he were there. My daughter went to bed imagining that her best friend of fifteen years was sleeping next to her bed as he always did.

Early the next morning, we discovered a notice on a tree at the foot of the mountains saying that someone had found a little dog. It was Cabbie. Just as we had imagined, our dog returned home safely to us.

No matter what challenging situation you may find yourself in, imagine the best outcome and feel it! When you do, you will change the circumstances, and you will change the situation into what you want!

Whatever You Can Imagine Exists

"Creation is only the projection into form of that which already exists."

Srimad Bhagavatam (9TH CENTURY)
ANCIENT HINDU TEXT

Whatever desire you can imagine – already exists! It doesn't matter what it is, if you can imagine it, it already exists in creation.

Five thousand years ago, ancient scriptures recorded that all of creation was done and complete, and that anything that could possibly be created already exists. Now, five thousand years later, quantum physics has confirmed that every single possibility of anything and everything actually exists *now*.

"The creation of the heavens and the earth and everything in them was complete."

Genesis 2:1

What that means for you and your life is that whatever you can imagine for yourself in your life already exists. It's impossible for you to imagine anything that doesn't exist. Creation is complete. Every single possibility exists. So when you imagine breaking a world record or traveling to the Far East or being full of health or being a parent, those possibilities of you doing those things exist in creation right now! If they didn't exist already, you would not be able to imagine them! To bring the things you desire and love from the invisible into your visible life, all you have to do is give love for what you want through your imagination and feelings.

Imagine your life the way you want it to be. Imagine everything you want. Take your imagination with you every day, and *imagine* what it would be like *if* your relationships were all wonderful. *Imagine* how you would feel *if* your job suddenly took off. *Imagine* how your life would be *if* you had the money you need to do what you love. *Imagine* how you would feel *if* you were overflowing with health. *Imagine* how you would feel *if* you could do what you wanted to do. Use all of your senses to imagine what you want. If you want to travel to Italy, imagine the smell of olive oil, taste the pasta, hear Italian words being spoken to you, touch the stone of the Colosseum, and *feel* being in Italy!

In conversations and in your thoughts say, "*Imagine if* . . ." and then fill in the rest of the sentence with what you want! If you're talking to a friend and they're complaining because their work colleague got a promotion and they didn't, help them by saying, "Imagine if the reason you didn't get that promotion is that you are being promoted to an even bigger role, with way more money!" Because the truth is that the possibility of your friend being promoted to an even bigger role with way more money already exists, and if they can imagine and feel it, they can receive it!

> *"Atoms or elementary particles themselves are not real; they form a world of potentialities or possibilities rather than one of things or facts."*
>
> *Werner Heisenberg* (1901-1976)
> NOBEL PRIZE—WINNING QUANTUM PHYSICIST

Use your imagination and create games so that you feel really good. Whatever you can imagine is waiting for you, fully created in the invisible, and the way to make it visible is to harness the force of love by imagining and feeling what you love.

After graduating from college, a young woman struggled for months and months trying to get a job. Her biggest obstacle was imagining having a job when she didn't have one. She wrote in her journal every day that she was grateful for the job that was coming to her, but still no job. Then she had a sudden realization. Her desperate actions of applying for one job after another were saying loud and clear to the law of attraction that she didn't have a job.

So here is what the young woman did that changed everything. She decided to use her imagination and live as though she were already employed. She set her alarm early as if she were going to work. Instead of writing in her journal that she was grateful for the job that was coming, she wrote how grateful she was for her success in her job and for the people she worked with. She planned the clothes she would wear to work each day. She set up a savings account for her paychecks. Within two weeks, she felt as though she really had a job. Then out of the blue, a friend told her about a position that had become available. She went for an interview, got the job, and received everything she had written about in her journal.

Prop Yourself Up

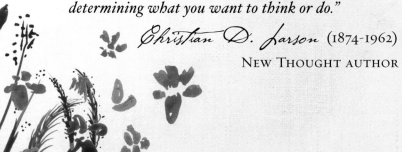

"Whenever you permit yourself to think what persons, things, conditions, or circumstances may suggest, you are not following what you want to think. You are not following your own desires but borrowed desires. Use your imagination in determining what you want to think or do."

Christian D. Larson (1874-1962)
NEW THOUGHT AUTHOR

When using the Creation Process, use all the props you can to generate the feeling that you have what you want already. Surround yourself with items of clothing, pictures, photographs, and relevant objects, so you can imagine and feel the feelings of having what you want.

If you want new clothes, make sure you have space in your wardrobe, with empty clothes hangers ready for your new clothes. If you want to bring more money into your life, does your wallet have space for money or is it full of irrelevant bits of paper? If you want the perfect partner, you must imagine and feel that the person is with you now. Are you sleeping in the middle of your bed, or are you sleeping on one side because your partner is on the other side of your bed? If your partner were with you now, you would be using only half the space in your wardrobe, because your partner's clothes would be in the other half of the wardrobe. Do you set your table for two people or one person? Just putting out an extra place is something you can easily do. Do your best not to contradict your desire in your day-to-day actions, and instead use the world of props that surround you to feel as though you already have what you want. These are simple little things you can do with props and your imagination, but they are incredibly powerful.

One woman used props and her imagination to receive a horse. She had wanted a horse all her life, but she could not afford to buy one. She wanted a chestnut Morgan gelding and a Morgan would cost thousands and thousands of dollars.

So she imagined seeing the exact horse she wanted each time she looked outside her kitchen window. She put a picture of a chestnut Morgan horse on the screen of her laptop computer. Whenever she had the opportunity, she doodled drawings of the horse. She began looking at horses for sale, even though she couldn't afford them. She took her children to a store and together they tried on riding boots. She looked at saddles. She bought the only things she could afford, a horse blanket, lead, and horse brushes, and she kept them on display so she could see them every day. Sometime later, the woman went to a horse expo in her town. A raffle was being held at the expo and the first prize was a chestnut Morgan gelding, the exact same horse she had been imagining! And of course she won the raffle and received her horse!

Your senses are props too. So use all your senses to help you feel that you have what you want. Feel the touch of what you want with your skin. Taste it, smell it, see it, and hear it!

One man worked with all his senses to bring himself multiple job offers. He had applied for 75 positions over three years and had not received a single job offer, but then he used his imagination and all his senses to imagine he had his dream job. He imagined every detail in his new office. He touched the keys of his computer in his imagination. He smelled the lemon scent of the furniture polish on his new huge mahogany desk. He imagined his work colleagues. He gave them names. He had conversations with them. He had meetings with them. He even tasted the tacos at lunch breaks. Seven weeks later he began receiving requests for interviews. Then requests for second interviews poured in. Then he received not only one fantastic job offer but two. He accepted the job he loved the most: it was his dream job!

Know that when you have completed your part in the Creation Process, creation is done! You are no longer in the old world where you didn't have what you wanted. You have moved into a new world that contains the very thing you want even if you can't see it yet. Know that you will receive it!

POINTS OF POWER

- *To harness the force of love in your life to bring something you want or change something you don't want, the Creation Process is always the same: Imagine it. Feel it. Receive it.*

- *Your imagination connects you to what you want. Your desire and feelings of love create the magnetism, the magnetic power, drawing your desire to you!*

- *Imagine yourself being with your desire. At the same time, feel love for what you're imagining.*

- *Desire what you want with all of your heart because desire is a feeling of love, and you must give love to receive what you love!*

- *When you imagine anything positive that you want and love, you are harnessing the force of love. Push your imagination to the limits, and imagine the best and highest that you possibly can of whatever it is that you want.*

- *Whatever desire you can imagine already exists! It doesn't matter what it is: if you can imagine it, it already exists in creation.*

- *In conversations and in your thoughts say, "Imagine if . . ." and then complete the sentence with what you want!*

- *Use props. Surround yourself with items of clothing, pictures, photographs, and relevant objects, so you can imagine and feel the feelings of having what you want.*

- *Your senses are props too. Use all your senses to help you feel that you have what you want. Feel it, taste it, smell it, see it, and hear it!*

- *When you have completed your part in the Creation Process, you have moved into a new world that contains the very thing you want even if you can't see it yet. Know you will receive it!*

FEELING IS CREATION

"Whenever your feeling is in conflict with your wish, feeling will be the victor."

Neville Goddard (1905-1972)
NEW THOUGHT AUTHOR

Fields of Feelings

I want you to understand what happens to you when you give love through your good feelings because it is truly magnificent. Your feelings create a magnetic field that completely surrounds you. Every person is surrounded by a magnetic field, and so wherever you go, the magnetic field goes with you. You may have seen ancient pictures depicting something similar where they show an aura or halo surrounding a person. Well, the aura surrounding each person is actually an electromagnetic field, and it's through the magnetism of your field that surrounds you that you attract everything in your life. What determines whether your field is positive or negative at any time is your feelings!

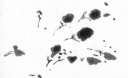

Every single time you give love, through your feelings, words, or actions, you add more love to the field around you. The more love you give, the greater and more powerful is your magnetic field. Whatever is in your magnetic field is attracting to itself, and so the more love in your field, the more power you have to attract the things you love. You can get to a point where the magnetic power in your field is so positive and strong that you can have a flash of imagining and feeling something good, and within no time, it has appeared in your life! That is the incredible power you have. And that is the phenomenal power of the force of love!

> *"Through your ability to think and feel, you have dominion over all creation."*
>
> *Neville Goddard* (1905-1972)
> NEW THOUGHT AUTHOR

I want to share a very simple situation that happened in my life that demonstrates how fast love can work. I love flowers and so I do my best to have fresh flowers each week because they make me feel happy. Usually I buy flowers from the farmer's market, but on this particular week it was raining and there was no farmer's market, and no flowers. My response to there being no flowers was that it was a really good thing because it would make me appreciate and love flowers even more. Instead of feeling disappointment, I chose to feel love, and so I filled my magnetic field with the love of flowers.

Within two hours I received a delivery of an enormous vase of flowers. From across the other side of the world, my sister had sent me the most beautiful flowers you have ever seen, thanking me for something I had done for her. When you can give love, no matter what the circumstances, the circumstances must change!

Now you can appreciate why it is so important to choose love, because every time you give love, you increase and multiply the love in the magnetic field around you. The more love you give in your day-to-day life, the greater the magnetic power of love you have in the field around you, and everything you want will fall at your feet.

This is the magic of what your life will be when you are giving love. My life did not used to be as magical as it is now. My life used to be full of struggle and difficulties, but I discovered something fantastic about life, and what I discovered is everything I am sharing with you in this book. Nothing is too big for the force of love. There is no distance too great, no obstacle it cannot overcome; time cannot stand in its way. You can change anything in your life by harnessing the greatest power in the universe, and all you have to do is give love!

The Point of Creation

You can tend to think of the things you want as really big things, but your perspective is way out of proportion when you think that way. When you think something is really big, in effect you're saying to the law of attraction, "This is so big it's going to be difficult to achieve, and it's probably going to take a really long time." And you will be right, because whatever you think and feel is what you will receive. If you think your desire is really big, you will create difficulty and a time delay in receiving what you want. But there is no big or small for the law of attraction, and there is no concept of time for the law of attraction.

To help you have the true perspective of creation, no matter how big your desire may seem to you, think of it as the size of a dot! You may want a house, car, vacation, money, the perfect partner, your dream job, or children. You may want to receive full health in your body. You may want to pass exams, get into a particular college, break a world record, become president, a successful actor, lawyer, writer, or teacher. It doesn't matter what it is you want, think of it as the size of a dot, because for the force of love, what you want is *smaller* than a dot!

"Our doubts are traitors and make us lose the good we oft might win."

William Shakespeare (1564-1616)
ENGLISH PLAYWRIGHT

If you find your faith wavering, just put a dot in the center of a large circle and next to the dot write the name of your desire. As often as you like, look at your drawing of the dot in the circle, knowing your desire *is* the size of that dot for the force of love!

How to Change Something Negative

If there is something negative in your life and you want to change it, the process is the same: Give love by imagining and feeling that you have what you want. Remember that anything negative is a lack of love, and so you have to imagine the opposite of the negative situation, because its opposite *is* love! For example, if you have an illness that you want to be gone, give love for your body being healthy.

If you are using the Creation Process to change something negative, know that you do not have to turn the negative into a positive. That feels really hard to do and it is not how creation works. Creation means something *new* is created – which automatically replaces the old. You don't need to think about what you want to change. All you have to do is give love for what you want, and the force of love will replace the negativity for you.

If a person is injured and receiving medical help, but things are not improving, it means they're imagining and feeling the injury more than they're imagining and feeling a full recovery. The way to tip the balance to recovery is to imagine and feel having a full recovery, *more* than not having it. The fact that you can imagine a full recovery means that it already exists! Impregnate your magnetic field with good feelings about anything and everything that makes you feel good. Ramp up your love in every area of your life.

Feel good as much as you can, because every moment of giving love brings a full recovery.

"Your feelings are your god."

Chanakya (350-275 BC)

INDIAN POLITICIAN AND WRITER

Whether you want to change your health, money, relationships, or anything else, the process is the same! Imagine what you want. Imagine and feel the love of having it. Imagine every scene and situation you can with what you want, and feel that you have it now. Try spending seven minutes each day imagining and feeling having what you want. Do it each day until you feel as though you already have your desire. Do it until you know your desire belongs to you, as you know your name belongs to you. With some things you will get to this state after just one or two days. Other things may take you longer. Then simply get on with your life, giving as much love and as many good feelings as you can *because the more love you give, the faster you will receive what you desire.*

After you've imagined and felt having what you want, you're literally in a new world with what you've imagined, so don't contradict the new world by telling everyone about an injury that's not improving, because then you are imagining the worst again, and you're back in the old world. As you imagine the worst, that's what you will receive back. As you imagine the best, that's what you'll receive back. If somebody asks how your injury is doing, you can say, "I am *feeling* one hundred percent again and my body is following." You can say, "This has been a blessing because it has made me appreciate my body and health more than I ever have in my life." Or if you are bold enough you can say, "I have a full recovery by the horns."

You can't talk about something you don't want without feeling bad. It's that simple, but people are so used to not feeling good a lot of the time, they don't even notice how bad they feel when they're imagining and talking about what they don't want. When you become more aware of how you're feeling, and you care more about your feelings, you will get to the point where the slightest dip in your good feelings will be unbearable for you. You will become so used to feeling good, you'll be so aware of your feelings, that if they dip you will feel it and you'll get yourself back to feeling good right away. You are supposed to feel good and be happy most of the time, because you are meant to have an amazing life, and there is no other way you can receive it!

*"I am still determined to be cheerful and happy,
in whatever situation I may be; for I have also
learned from experience that the greater part
of our happiness or misery depends upon our
dispositions, and not upon our circumstances."*

Martha Washington (1732–1802)

FIRST LADY, WIFE OF GEORGE WASHINGTON,
FIRST PRESIDENT OF THE UNITED STATES

How to Eliminate Bad Feelings

You can change anything in your life by changing how
you feel. When you change how you feel about any subject,
the subject must change! But in changing the way you feel,
don't try to get rid of bad feelings, because all bad feelings are
simply a lack of love. Instead, you put love in! You don't try to
get rid of anger or sadness; anger and sadness are gone when
you put love in. There is nothing to dig out of you. When you
put love into you, all bad feelings are gone.

There is only one force in life and that force is love. You
are either feeling good because you are full of love, or you are
feeling bad because you are empty of love, but all your feelings
are degrees of love.

Think of love as if it is water in a glass, and the glass
is your body. When a glass has only a little water in it, it is

empty of water. You can't change the water level in the glass by waging war on the emptiness and trying to rip out the emptiness. The emptiness goes by filling the glass with water. When you have bad feelings, you are empty of love, and so when you put love into yourself, the bad feelings are gone.

Don't Resist Bad Feelings

Everything has its perfect place in life, including bad feelings. Without bad feelings, you would never know what it feels like to feel good. You would just feel the one "blah" feeling all the time because you would have nothing to compare your feelings to. You wouldn't know what it feels like to feel really happy, excited, or joyful. It's through feeling sadness that you know how good it feels to be happy. You can never remove bad feelings from life because they are a part of life, and without them, you wouldn't have good feelings!

If you feel bad about having bad feelings, you are adding more power to your bad feelings. Not only will your bad feelings get worse, but you will increase the negativity you're giving out. Now you understand that bad feelings don't bring the life you want, which will make you more mindful not to let bad feelings take over you. You are in charge of your feelings, and so if you have a bad feeling sweeping over you, one way to discharge its energy is to lighten up!

> *"There is a world within – a world of thought and feeling and power; of light and beauty, and although invisible, its forces are mighty."*
>
> *Charles Haanel* (1866-1949)
> NEW THOUGHT AUTHOR

Life is supposed to be fun! When you're having fun, you feel great and you receive great things! When you take life too seriously, you receive serious things. Having fun brings the life you want, and taking things too seriously brings a life you have to take seriously. You have the power over your life, and you can use it to design your life in whatever way you want, but for your own sake, lighten up!

To lighten up about bad feelings, I have imagined bad feelings as wild horses. There's an angry horse, a resentful horse, blaming horse, sulky horse, cranky horse, grumpy horse, an irritable horse – you name it, there's a stable full of bad feeling horses. If I feel some disappointment over something that has happened, then I say to myself, "Why did you climb on the disappointment horse? Get off it now, because it's heading for *more* disappointment and you don't want to go where it's going." And so I imagine bad feelings as wild horses I climb on, and if I climbed on them, then I can get off them too. I don't see bad feelings as something that is the real me or anyone else, because that is not the truth. Bad feelings are not who you are, and they are not who anyone is. A bad feeling is something you allowed yourself to feel, and you can choose to get off that horse as fast as you jumped on to it.

If you think of bad feelings as a wild horse that you climbed on, it's one way to take the power out of bad feelings! If someone close to you is cranky, their bad feeling will have far less power to affect you if you imagine them as having climbed on a cranky horse. You will not take their crankiness so personally. But if you do take it personally and you become cranky from their crankiness, then *you* just jumped on the cranky horse with them!

"Respond intelligently even to unintelligent treatment."

Lao Tzu (CIRCA 6TH CENTURY BC)
FOUNDER OF TAOISM

And so with anything in life that I don't want, I use my imagination to have fun and take the power out of what I don't want. Sometimes watching myself or other people ride wild horses in various life situations makes me laugh, and when you can laugh yourself out of a bad feeling, that is really something! You have just changed your life.

So if you are feeling bad, don't give that bad feeling more power by beating up on yourself that you feel bad. If you do that, you're just whipping the wild horse into a bigger negative frenzy. The idea is not to hate bad feelings but to deliberately choose good feelings, and choose them more often. When you resist bad feelings, they increase! The more you don't want bad feelings, the more you increase them. The more you resist anything in life, the more you bring it to you. So don't care about bad feelings if they come upon you. Don't resist them at all, and then you take all the power out of them.

POINTS OF POWER

- *Every person is surrounded by a magnetic field. Wherever you go, the magnetic field goes with you.*

- *You attract everything through the magnetism of your field. Your feelings determine whether your field is positive or negative at any time.*

- *Every single time you give love, through your feelings, words, or actions, you add more love to the field around you.*

- *The more love in your field, the more power you have to attract the things you love.*

- *Imagine what you want as the size of a dot! For the force of love, what you want is smaller than a dot!*

- *You do not have to turn the negative into a positive. Just give love for what you want, because the creation of what you want replaces the negativity!*

- *Spend seven minutes each day imagining and feeling having what you want. Do it until you know your desire belongs to you, as you know your name belongs to you.*

- *There is only one force in life and that force is love. You are either feeling good because you are full of love, or you are feeling bad because you are empty of love – but all of your feelings are degrees of love.*

- *To lighten up about bad feelings, imagine bad feelings as wild horses you climb on. If you climbed on them you can climb off them, too! You can choose to get off that horse as fast as you jumped on to it.*

- *Change what you give, and you will always, without exception, change what you receive, because that is the law of attraction. That is the law of love.*

LIFE FOLLOWS YOU . . .

"Destiny is no matter of chance. It is a matter of choice."

William Jennings Bryan (1860-1925)
UNITED STATES POLITICAL LEADER

Life *follows* you. Absolutely everything you experience in your life is a result of what you have given out in your thoughts and feelings, whether you realize you have given them or not. Life is not happening *to* you . . . life is *following* you. Your destiny is in your hands. Whatever you think, whatever you feel, will decide your life.

Everything in life is presented to you for you to choose what *you* love! Life is a catalogue, and you are the one who chooses what you love from the catalogue! But are you choosing the things you love or are you too busy judging and labeling the bad things? If your life is far from wonderful, then you've inadvertently been labeling all the bad things. You've allowed the things you think are bad to distract you from the purpose of your life. Because the purpose of your life is to love! The purpose of your life is joy. The purpose of your life

is to choose the things you love and turn away from the things
you don't love so you don't choose them.

Choose What You Love

When you see your dream car go whizzing down the
street, life is presenting that car to you! How you feel when
you see your dream car is everything, because if you choose to
feel nothing but love for that car, you are bringing your dream
car to you. But if you feel envy or jealousy because someone
else is driving your dream car, you just gonged yourself out of
having your dream car. Life presented the car to you so you
could choose. And you choose it, by feeling love. Do you see
that it doesn't matter whether someone else has something
and you don't? Life is presenting everything to you, and if you
feel love for it, you are bringing the same thing to you.

When you see a happy couple madly in love, and you
desperately want a partner in your life, life is presenting the
happy couple to you – for you to choose. But if you feel sad
or lonely when you see the happy couple, you just gave out
negativity, and in effect said, "I want to be sad and lonely." You
have to give love for what you want. If you are overweight and
you're walking down the street and a person with a perfect
body passes you by, how do you feel? Life is presenting the
great body to you for you to choose, and so if you feel bad
because you don't have that body, you just said, "I don't want a
body like that, I want the overweight body I have." If you are

struggling with some kind of disease, and you are surrounded by healthy people, how do you feel? Life is presenting healthy people to you so you can choose health, and so when you feel love for the health around you, more than you feel bad about a lack of health, you are choosing health for yourself.

When you feel good about anything any person has, you are bringing it to you. When you feel good about the success of another person, the happiness of another person, or all the good things anyone else has, you are choosing those things from the catalogue of life, and you are bringing them to yourself.

If you meet someone who has qualities you wish you had, love those qualities and feel good about those qualities in that person, and you are bringing those qualities to yourself. If someone is smart, beautiful, or talented, love those qualities and you choose those things for *you*!

If you want to become a parent and you've been trying for a long time, then give love and feel good every single time you see a parent with a child! If you feel depressed when you see children because you don't have a child, then you are repelling and pushing children away from you. Life is presenting children to you each time you see them, so you can choose.

When you're playing a sport and another person wins, when a work colleague tells you they got a pay raise, when someone wins the lottery, when a friend tells you that their spouse gave them a surprise gift of a weekend away, or that they bought a beautiful new house, or that their child won a scholarship, you should be as excited as they are. You should be as excited and happy as though it has happened to you, because then you are saying yes to it, then you are giving love to it, and you are bringing it to you!

When you see your dream car, a happy couple, the perfect body, children, great qualities in a person, or whatever it is you want, it means you are on the same frequency as those things! Be excited, because your excitement is choosing it.

Everything in life is presenting itself to you so you can choose what you love and what you don't love, but only love brings what you want to you. Life's catalogue contains many things you don't love, so don't choose them by giving bad feelings. Judge another person and think they're bad, and you bring negativity to you. Feel envious or jealous of something another person has, and you bring negativity to you while pushing away the very thing you want with a mighty force. Only love brings what you want to you!

"This is the miracle that happens every time to those who really love: the more they give, the more they possess."

Rainer Maria Rilke (1875-1926)

AUTHOR AND POET

The Law of One – You!

There is a simple formula you can use for the law of
attraction that will stand you in good stead with every person,
situation, and circumstance. As far as the law of attraction
is concerned, there is only one person in the world – you!
There is no other person, and nothing else as far as the law of
attraction is concerned. There is only you, because the law of
attraction is responding to *your* feelings! It's only what *you* give
that counts. And it's the same for every other person. And so
in truth the law of attraction is the law of *you*. There is only
you, and there is no other person. For the law of attraction the
other person is you, and that other person is you, and those
other people are you, because whatever you feel about anyone
else, you are bringing to *you*.

What you feel about another person, what you think or say about another person, what you do to another person – you do to you. Give judgment and criticism and you give it to yourself. Give love and appreciation to another person or anything, and you give it to yourself. There is no other for the law of attraction, so it makes no difference if someone else has what you want, when you feel love for it you're including it in *your* life! And with anything you don't love, simply turn away from it without judgment, and you won't include it in your life.

There Is Only Yes for the Law of Attraction

Turn away from the things you don't love and don't give them any feeling. Don't say no to the things you don't love, because saying no brings them to you. When you say no to the things you don't love, you're feeling bad about them, you're giving bad feelings, and you will receive those feelings back as negative circumstances in your life.

You can't say no to anything, because when you say, "No I don't want that," you are saying *yes* to the law of attraction. When you say, "The traffic is terrible," "The service is really bad," "They're always late," "It's so noisy in here," "That driver is a lunatic," "I've been on hold for so long," you are saying *yes* to these things and you are including more of all of them in your life.

Turn away from the things you don't love and don't give them any feeling, because they are fine as they are but they have no place in your life.

"See no evil – hear no evil – speak no evil."
Maxim on the Toshogu Shrine in Japan
(17TH CENTURY)

Instead say *yes* when you see something you love. Say *yes* when you hear something you love. Say *yes* when you taste something you love. Say *yes* when you smell something you love. Say *yes* when you touch something you love. It doesn't matter if you have it or not, say *yes* to it, because then you are choosing it by giving love.

There are no limits, and everything is possible if you really want it, if you really desire it. There is no lack anywhere in the universe. When people see a lack of anything, it's simply a lack of love. There isn't a lack of health, money, resources or happiness. The supply is equal to the demand. Give love, and you will receive!

Your Life – Your Story

You are creating the story of your life, so what story are you telling about yourself? Do you believe there are things you can and cannot do? Is that the story you are telling about yourself? Because that story is not true.

Don't listen if someone says you are less than anyone else. Don't listen if someone says you are limited in any way. Don't listen if someone says you can't do what you love to do and earn a living from it. Don't listen if someone says you are not as valuable and worthy as the greatest human beings who've lived. Don't listen if someone says you are not good enough now and you have to prove yourself in life. Don't listen if someone says you can't have what you love or do what you love or be what you love. If you believe it, you put limits on yourself, but more importantly, it is not true! There is not a single thing that is too good for you, or too good to be true.

The force of love says, "Whatever you give, you receive back." Does that say you're not good enough? The force of love says, "Give love for whatever you want to be, do, or have and you will receive it." Does that say you're not good enough? You are worthy and deserving just as you are. You *are* good enough now. If you feel you have done something that wasn't right, understand that your *realization* and *acceptance* of it is absolution for the law of attraction.

The Real World

"In the beginning there were only probabilities. The universe could only come into existence if someone observed it. It does not matter that the observers turned up several billion years later. The universe exists because we are aware of it."

Martin Rees (B. 1942)
ASTROPHYSICIST

I want to take you behind the scenes of the world you see, because much of what you see is not as real as you may think it is. A few adventurous steps into the invisible will change the way you look at the world, and it will set you free to receive an unlimited life.

Most of the things you may currently believe about the real world are not true. You are much more than you may realize. Life and the universe are much more than you may realize. You may think there is a limited amount of things in the world. You may think there's a limited amount of money, health, and resources, but it isn't true. There is no lack of anything. Quantum physics tell us there are infinite planet Earths and infinite universes that exist, and we move from one reality of planet Earth and a universe to another, every fraction of a second. This is the real world emerging through science.

"In our universe we are tuned into the frequency that corresponds to physical reality. But there are an infinite number of parallel realities coexisting with us in the same room, although we cannot tune into them."

Steven Weinberg (B. 1933)
NOBEL PRIZE–WINNING QUANTUM PHYSICIST

You may think there's a shortage of time in the real world, and because of that you may live your life rushing against time, but the great scientist Albert Einstein told us that time is an illusion.

"The distinction between past, present, and future is only a stubbornly persistent illusion."

Albert Einstein (1879-1955)
NOBEL PRIZE–WINNING PHYSICIST

You may think that the real world is made up of living things and dead things. But in the universe *everything* is alive and *nothing* is dead. The stars, sun, planets, earth, air, water, fire, and every object you see is seething with life. This is the real world that is emerging.

"There is a sense in the tree which feels your love and responds to it. It does not respond or show its pleasure in our way or in any way we can now understand."

Prentice Mulford (1834-1891)
NEW THOUGHT AUTHOR

You may believe the real world is everything you can see, and that everything you can't see isn't real. And yet the color you see when you look at something is in fact *not* its real color. Each thing absorbs all the colors that it really is, and reflects the color it is not, and that's the color you see. So the sky is actually every color *but* blue!

There are many sounds you can't hear because their frequencies are beyond what you can hear, but they are real. You can't see ultraviolet or infrared light, because their frequencies are beyond what your eye can see, but they are real. If you imagine all the known frequencies of light as the size of Mount Everest, then all that you can see is smaller than a golf ball!

You may believe the real world is made up of all the solid things you can see and touch. But actually nothing is solid! The chair you're sitting on right now is a force of moving energy, and it's mostly space. So how real is your chair?

"A wise man, recognizing that the world is but an illusion, does not act as if it is real, so (therefore) he escapes the suffering."

Gautama Buddha (563-483 BC)

FOUNDER OF BUDDHISM

You may believe that your imagination is just thoughts and dreams and has no power in the real world. And yet one of the hurdles for scientists in proving things to be true or not is removing the scientist's beliefs from scientific experiments, because what the scientist believes or imagines will be the outcome of an experiment *affects* the outcome of the experiment. This is the power of human imagination and beliefs! Just as the scientist's beliefs affect the outcome of an experiment, so do your beliefs affect the outcome of your life.

Your beliefs, true or untrue, form your world. What you imagine and *feel* to be true creates your life, because that is what you're giving to the law of attraction, and that is what will be returned to you. Your imagination is more real than the world you see, because the world you see comes from what you imagine and believe! What you believe and *feel* to be true is what will be your life. If you believe you can't have the life you dream of, then the law of attraction must follow what you say, and that will be your real world.

*"To believe in the things you can see and touch
is no belief at all; but to believe in the unseen
is a triumph and a blessing."*

Abraham Lincoln (1809-1865)
16TH PRESIDENT OF THE UNITED STATES

A story of limitation has been passed on from one generation to the next through the history of humanity, but the time has come to tell the real story.

The Real Story

The real story is that you are an unlimited being. The real story is that the world and the universe are unlimited. There are worlds and possibilities that you cannot see, but all of them exist. You have to start telling a different story! You have to start telling the story of your amazing life, because whatever story you tell, good or bad, the law of attraction must make sure you receive it, and it will be the story of your life.

Imagine and *feel* whatever you want and those will be the pictures you receive back in your life. Give love as much as you can and feel as good as you can, and the force of love will surround you with people, circumstances, and events that you love. You can be whatever you want. You can do whatever you want. You can have whatever you want.

What do you love? What do you want?

Let go of anything you don't love about your life story and just keep the things you love. If you hold on to negative things from your past, then you keep putting them into your story every time you remember them, and they go back into the pictures of your life – now!

Let go of the things you don't love about your childhood, and keep the things you love. Let go of the things you don't love about your adolescent and adult years, and keep the good things. Just keep the things you love about your whole life. All the negative things of the past are done, finished; you are not the same person as you were then, so why keep putting them in your story if they make you feel bad? You don't have to dig negative things out of you from the past. Just don't put them in your story anymore.

"A mighty, eternal and incomprehensible force pushes us all forward. But while all are so being pushed, many linger and look back. Unconsciously, they oppose this force."

Prentice Mulford (1834-1891)
NEW THOUGHT AUTHOR

If you keep telling a story of being a victim, then those pictures will play over and over again in your life. If you keep telling a story that you're not as smart as other people, or not as attractive as other people, or not as talented as other people, you will be right because they will become the pictures of your life.

When you fill your life with love, you'll find that guilt, resentment, and any negative feelings will leave you. And then you will start telling the greatest story ever told, and the force of love will light up your life with the pictures of the *real* story of your amazing life.

"Love is the greatest power on earth. It conquers all things."

Peace Pilgrim
BORN MILDRED LISETTE NORMAN (1908-1981)
PEACE ACTIVIST

POINTS OF POWER

- *Life presents everything to you for you to choose what you love!*

- *If someone has something you want, be as excited as though you have it. If you feel love for it, you are bringing the same thing to you.*

- *When you see the things you want, you are on the same frequency as those things!*

- *Life's catalogue contains things you don't love, so don't choose them by giving bad feelings.*

- *Turn away from the things you don't love and don't give them any feeling. Instead say yes when you see something you love.*

- *The law of attraction is responding to your feelings! It's only what you give that counts. The law of attraction – is the law of you.*

- *Give judgment and criticism and you give it to yourself. Give love and appreciation to another person or anything, and you give it to yourself.*

- *When people see a lack of anything, it's simply a lack of love.*

- *You are good enough now. If you have done something that wasn't right, your realization and acceptance of it is absolution for the law of attraction.*

- *It's your beliefs, true or untrue, that form your world.*

- *Your imagination is more real than the world you see, because the world you see comes from what you imagine and believe! What you believe and feel to be true is what will be your life.*

- *Whatever story you tell, whether good or bad, will be the story of your life. So start telling the story of your amazing life, and the law of attraction must make sure you receive it.*

KEYS TO POWER

"Your most precious, valued possessions and your greatest powers are invisible and intangible. No one can take them. You, and you alone, can give them. You will receive abundance for your giving."

W. Clement Stone (1902-2002)

AUTHOR AND BUSINESSMAN

The Keys to Power are the most powerful ways to harness the force of love and receive the life you are meant to live. They are so simple and easy any child can follow them. Each key will unlock the immense power within you.

The Key of Love

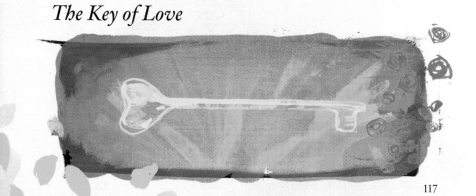

To use love as the ultimate power in your life, you must love like you have never loved before. Fall in love with life! However much you have loved in your life, double that feeling, multiply that feeling by ten times, multiply it by a hundred times, a thousand times, and a million times, because that is the level of love you are capable of feeling! There is no limit, no ceiling, to the amount of love you can feel and it is all inside you! You are made of love. It is the very substance and nature of you, life, and the universe, and you can love far more than you've ever loved before, and far more than you have imagined.

When you fall in love with life, every limitation disappears. You break the limitations on money, health, happiness, and the limits of joy in your relationships. When you fall in love with life, you have no resistance, and whatever you love appears in your life almost instantaneously. Your presence will be felt when you walk into a room. Opportunities will pour into your life, and your slightest touch will dissolve negativity. You will feel better than you thought it was possible to feel. You will be filled with unlimited energy, excitement, and an unquenchable zest for life. You will feel as light as a feather, like you're floating on air, and everything you love will just seem to fall at your feet. Fall in love with life, unleash the power within you, and you will become unlimited and invincible!

*"Even after all this time, the sun never says to
the earth, 'You owe me.' Look what happens with
a Love like that! It lights the whole sky."*

Hafez (1315-1390)

SUFI POET

So how do you fall in love with life? The same way you
fall in love with another person – you adore *everything* about
them! You fall in love with another person by seeing only love,
hearing only love, speaking only love, and by *feeling* love with
all your heart! And that is exactly how you use the ultimate
power of love to fall in love with life.

Whatever you're doing, wherever you are in your day,
look for the things you love. You can look for technology and
inventions you love. Look for buildings you love, cars and
roads you love, cafes and restaurants you love, stores you love.
Walk down a street or through a store with the intention
of finding as many things as you can that you love. Look for
things you love about other people. Look for everything you
love in nature – birds, trees, flowers, perfumes, and the colors
of nature. See what you love. Hear what you love. Speak about
what you love.

"Knowing that you have working with you a force, which never yet has failed in anything it has undertaken, you can go ahead in the confident knowledge that it will not fail in your case, either."

Robert Collier (1885-1950)

NEW THOUGHT AUTHOR

Think about what you love. Talk about what you love. Do what you love to do. Because when you're doing all of these things, you are *feeling* love.

Talk about the things you love about your home, your family, your spouse, and children. Talk about the things you love about your friends. Tell them what you love about them. Talk about the things you touch, smell, and taste that you love.

Tell the law of attraction what you love every day by singling out the things you love and feeling them. Just think about how much love you can give in one day by feeling the things you love. When you walk down the street, look for the things you love in other people. When you look in stores, look for the things you love. Say, "I love that outfit," "I love those shoes," "I love the color of that person's eyes," "I love that person's hair," "I love that person's smile," "I love those cosmetics," "I love that smell," "I love this store," "I love that table, lamp, couch, rug, sound equipment, coat, gloves, tie, hat, and jewelry," "I love the smell of summer," "I love the trees in fall," "I love the flowers in spring," "I love that color," "I love this street," "I love this city."

Look for the things you love in situations, events, and circumstances, and *feel* those things. "I love getting phone calls like that." "I love getting emails like that." "I love hearing good news like that." "I love this song." "I love seeing people happy." "I love laughing with other people." "I love driving to work listening to music." "I love being able to relax on the train or the bus." "I love the festivals in my city." "I love celebrations." "I love life." Look for the things you love on every subject that lights up your heart, and feel the deepest love you can.

If you're not feeling good and you want to change the way you feel, or if you want to lift good feelings higher, then take a minute or two and go through a mental list of everything you love and adore. You can do it while getting dressed in the morning, walking, driving, or traveling anywhere. It's such a simple thing to do, but the effect in your life will be amazing.

Make a written list of everything you love, which I urge you to do every month in the beginning, and then at least every three months. Include the places you love, the cities, the countries, the people you love, colors you love, styles you love, qualities in people you love, companies you love, services you love, sports you love, athletes you love, music you love, animals you love, flowers, plants, and trees you love. List all the material things you love, from all the different types of clothes you love, homes, furniture, books, magazines, newspapers, cars, appliances, to all the different foods you love. Think about the things you love to do and list them all, such as dancing, playing a sport, going to galleries, concerts, parties, shopping, list the movies you love, vacations and restaurants you love.

> *"When one has once fully entered the realm of love, the world – no matter how imperfect – becomes rich and beautiful – it consists solely of opportunities for love."*
>
> *Søren Aabye Kierkegaard* (1813-1855)
> PHILOSOPHER

• Your job is to love as much as possible every day. If you can just love and adore everything you possibly can today, look for and feel the things you love, and turn away from the things you don't love, your tomorrows will overflow with the untold happiness of everything you want and love.

> *"Love is the master key that opens the gates of happiness."*
>
> *Oliver Wendell Holmes* (1809-1894)
> DEAN OF HARVARD MEDICAL SCHOOL

Love Is Being Alert

You have to be alert to feel the love of everything around you. You have to be aware of everything that's around you to love, otherwise you will miss things. You have to be alert to see the things that you love. You have to be alert to hear the sounds that you love. You have to be alert to catch the beautiful smells of flowers as you walk past them. You have to be alert to really taste the food you're eating and feel the fullness of the flavors. If you are walking down the street listening to the thoughts in your head, you miss it all. And that's what happens to people a lot of the time. They hypnotize themselves by listening to the thoughts in their head, and so they're in a kind of trance, and they're not aware of anything around them.

Have you ever been walking down the street and suddenly a good friend yelled out your name and you were startled because you hadn't seen him? Or maybe you saw a friend, and you had to call out her name a couple of times, and suddenly she jumped with a start when she saw you? Your calling her name woke her up because she was not aware of being on the street, but was lost in a trance, listening to the thoughts in her head. Have you ever been in a car traveling, and suddenly you looked around and realized you were close to your destination, but you didn't remember traveling a big part of the distance? You had hypnotized yourself by listening to your thoughts, and you were lost in a trance.

The good news is that the more you give love, the more alert and aware you will become! Love brings complete alertness. As you make a conscientious effort to notice as many things around you that you love as you can each day, you will become more aware and alert.

How to Keep Your Mind Focused on Love

> *"Clarity of mind means clarity of passion, too;*
> *this is why a great and clear mind loves ardently*
> *and sees distinctly what it loves."*
>
> *Blaise Pascal* (1623–1662)
>
> MATHEMATICIAN AND PHILOSOPHER

One way to stay alert is to trick your mind by asking questions such as "What can I see that I love?" "How many things can I see that I love?" "What else is there that I love?" "What can I see that thrills me?" "What can I see that excites me?" "What can I see that I'm passionate about?" "Are there more things I can see that I love?" "What can I hear that I love?" When you ask your mind questions, your mind can't help itself and it gets busy right away to give you the answers. It stops other thoughts immediately so as to come up with the answers to your questions.

The secret is to keep asking your mind questions regularly. The more questions you can ask, the more you will be in control of your mind. Your mind will be working with you and doing what you want it to do, instead of working against you.

Sometimes your mind can take off like a freight train down a mountain without a driver, if you don't stay in control of it. You are the driver of your mind, so take charge and keep it busy with your instructions by telling it where you want it to go. Your mind only takes off on its own if you're not telling it what to do.

> *"The mind acts like an enemy for those who don't control it."*
>
> *Bhagavad Gita* (5TH CENTURY BC)
> ANCIENT HINDU TEXT

Your mind is a powerful and magnificent tool you can use, but you must be in control of it. Rather than letting it distract you with out-of-control thoughts, you want your mind to help you give love. It doesn't take long to train your mind to focus on love, and once you have just watch what happens to your life!

The Key of Gratitude

"You cannot exercise much power without gratitude because it is gratitude that keeps you connected with power."

Wallace Wattles (1860–1911)

New Thought author

I know of thousands of people in the worst imaginable situations who have changed their lives completely through gratitude. I know of miracles that have taken place in health where there seemed to be no hope: failed kidneys regenerate, diseased hearts heal, eyesight is restored, tumors disappear, and bones grow and rebuild themselves. I know of broken relationships that have transformed into magnificent ones through gratitude: failed marriages completely restored, estranged family members reunited, parents transforming relationships with children and teenagers, and teachers transforming students. I have seen people who were in total poverty become wealthy through gratitude: people turned around failing businesses, and people who had struggled with money all their lives created abundance. Someone even went from living on the streets to having a job and a home in a week. I know of people who were in depression who catapulted into joyful and fulfilling lives through gratitude. People who have suffered from anxiety and every kind of mental illness have restored themselves to perfect mental health through gratitude.

Every single savior of the world used gratitude, because they all knew that gratitude was one of the highest expressions of love. They knew that when they were grateful, they were living in exact accordance with the law. Why do you think Jesus said *thank you* before he performed every miracle?

Every time you feel grateful you are *giving* love, and whatever you give, you receive. Whether you're giving thanks to a person or feeling grateful for a car, a vacation, a sunset, a gift, a new house, or an exciting event, you are giving love for those things, and you will receive back more joy, more health, more money, more amazing experiences, more incredible relationships, more opportunities.

Try it now. Think of something or someone you're grateful for. You could choose the person you love more than anyone else in the world. Focus on that person and think about all the things you love and are grateful for about that person. Then, in your mind or out loud, tell that person all those things you love and are grateful for about them, as though they were there with you. Tell them all the reasons you love them. You can recall particular instances or moments by saying, "Remember the time when . . ." As you're doing it, feel the gratitude begin to fill your heart and body.

The love you gave in that simple exercise must and will return to you in the relationship, and in your whole life. That is how easy it is to give love through gratitude.

Albert Einstein was one of the greatest scientists who ever lived. His discoveries completely changed the way we see the universe. And when asked about his monumental achievements, Einstein spoke only of giving thanks to others. One of the most brilliant minds that has ever lived thanked others for what they had given to him – a hundred times a day! That means at least a hundred times a day, Einstein gave love. Is it any wonder that life revealed so many of its mysteries to Albert Einstein?

"A hundred times every day I remind myself that my inner and outer life depend on the labors of other men, living and dead, and that I must exert myself in order to give in the same measure as I have received and am still receiving."

Albert Einstein (1879-1955)
NOBEL PRIZE–WINNING PHYSICIST

Gratitude, the Great Multiplier

When you're grateful for the things you have, no matter how small they may be, you will receive more of those things. If you're grateful for the money you have, however little, you will receive more money. If you're grateful for a relationship, even if it's not perfect, the relationship will get better. If you're grateful for the job that you have, even if it's not your dream job, you will receive better opportunities in your work. Because gratitude is the great multiplier of life!

"If the only prayer you say in your entire life is – 'thank you' – that is enough."

Meister Eckhart (1260-1328)
CHRISTIAN WRITER AND THEOLOGIAN

Gratitude begins with two simple words – *thank you* – but you have to feel grateful with all your heart. The more you start to say *thank you*, the more you will feel it, and the more love you will give. There are three ways to use the power of gratitude in your life, and every one of them is giving love:

1. *Be grateful for everything you have received in your life (past).*

2. *Be grateful for everything you are receiving in your life (present).*

3. *Be grateful for what you want in your life, as though you have received it (future).*

If you're not grateful for what you've received, and what you're receiving, you're not giving love, and you don't have the power to change any of your current circumstances. When you give thanks for what you've received and what you're continuing to receive, it *multiplies* those things. At the same time, gratitude brings what you want! Be grateful for what you want in your life, as though you have received it, and the law of attraction says you *must* receive it.

Can you imagine that something so simple as being grateful can multiply everything you love and completely change your life?

A divorced man, lonely, depressed, and working in a job he hated, decided to practice love and gratitude every day to change his life. He began by being positive to everyone he talked to during the day. When he called old friends and family, he shocked them with how positive and happy he was. He began to be grateful for everything he had, right down to being grateful for running water. This is what happened to his life within 120 days: Everything he hated about his job miraculously changed, and he now loves his job. His job even takes him to places that he has always wanted to see. He has the best relationships with all his family members, which he'd never had before. He paid off his car and he always has the money he needs. He has good days no matter what is happening. And he is married again – to his first love from tenth grade!

> *"Gratitude for the abundance you have received is the best insurance that the abundance will continue."*

Muhammad (570-632)

FOUNDER OF ISLAM

If you use gratitude a little, your life will change a little. If you use gratitude a lot every day, your life will change in ways you can hardly imagine now. Not only does gratitude multiply everything in your life, it also eliminates the negative things. No matter what negative situation you may find yourself in, you can *always* find something to be grateful for, and as you do, you harness the force of love that eliminates negativity.

Gratitude Is the Bridge to Love

"If we will be quiet and ready enough, we shall find compensation in every disappointment."

Henry David Thoreau (1817-1862)

TRANSCENDENTALIST AUTHOR

Gratitude took my mother from the deepest grief into happiness. My mother and father fell in love with each other virtually at first sight, and they had the most beautiful love affair and marriage I have ever seen. When my father died, my mother suffered from enormous grief, because she missed my father so much. But amidst her grief and pain, my mother began to look for things to be grateful for. Other than being grateful for all she had received from the decades of love and happiness with my father, she looked for things to be grateful for in the future. The first thing she found to be grateful for was that now she could travel. Traveling was something my mother had always wanted to do but didn't do when my father was alive, because he never wanted to travel. My mother did fulfill her dream; she traveled, and she did many other things that she had always wanted to do. Gratitude was the bridge that took my mother out of immense grief and into building a new life of happiness.

It's impossible to feel sad or have any negative feeling when you're grateful. If you're in the midst of a difficult situation, look for something to be grateful for. When you find one thing, then look for another, and then another, because every single thing you find to be grateful for changes the situation. Gratitude is the bridge from negative feelings to harnessing the force of love!

> *"Gratitude is a vaccine, an antitoxin, and an antiseptic."*
>
> *John Henry Jowett* (1864-1923)
> PRESBYTERIAN PREACHER AND AUTHOR

When anything good happens to you in your day, give thanks. It doesn't matter how small it is, say *thank you*. When you get the perfect parking space, hear your favorite song on the radio, approach a light that turns green, or find an empty seat on the bus or train, say *thank you*. These are all good things you're receiving from life.

Give thanks for your senses: your eyes that see, your ears that hear, your mouth that tastes, your nose that smells, and your skin that lets you feel. Give thanks for the legs you walk on, your hands that you use to do almost everything, your voice that enables you to express yourself and communicate with others. Give thanks for your amazing immune system that keeps you well or heals you, and for all your organs that maintain your body immaculately so that you can live. Give thanks for the magnificence of your human mind that no computer technology in the world can duplicate. Your entire body is the greatest laboratory on the planet, and there's nothing that can come even close to replicating its magnificence. You are a miracle!

Give thanks for your home, your family, your friends, your work, and your pets. Give thanks for the sun, the water that you drink, the food that you eat, and the air that you breathe; without any of them you wouldn't be alive.

Give thanks for the trees, the animals, the oceans, the birds, the flowers, the plants, blue skies, rain, the stars, the moon, and our beautiful planet.

Give thanks for the transportation you use every day. Give thanks for all the companies that provide you with essential services so that you can live a comfortable life. So many human beings toiled and sweated so that you can turn on a tap and have fresh water. So many human beings gave their life's work so that you can flick a light switch and have electricity. Think about the magnitude of human beings who slaved day after day, year after year, to lay the train tracks across our planet. And it's almost impossible to imagine the number of people who did the backbreaking work of making the roads we drive on that form a connecting network of life for the world.

"In ordinary life we hardly realize that we receive a great deal more than we give, and that it is only with gratitude that life becomes rich."

Dietrich Bonhoeffer (1906-1945)
LUTHERAN PASTOR

To use the power of gratitude, practice it. The more you *feel* gratitude, the more love you *give*; and the more love you give, the more you *receive*.

Are you grateful for your health when it's good? Or do you only notice your health when your body gets sick or hurts?

Are you grateful when you have a good night's sleep? Or do you take those nights for granted and only think of sleep when you've been deprived of it?

Are you grateful for your loved ones when everything is going well, or do you only talk about your relationships when there are problems?

Are you grateful for electricity when you use an appliance or flick a switch? Or do you only think of electricity when there's a power blackout?

Are you grateful to be alive each day?

Every spare second is an opportunity to be grateful and multiply the things you love. I used to think I was a grateful person, but I didn't know what gratitude really was until I practiced it.

If I am driving or walking I use the time to give thanks for everything in life. Even walking from my kitchen to my bedroom I will give thanks. With my heart I say, "Thank you for my life. Thank you for the harmony. Thank you for the joy. Thank you for my health. Thank you for the fun and excitement. Thank you for the wonder of life. Thank you for everything wonderful and good in my life."

Be grateful! Gratitude costs you nothing, but it is worth more than all the riches in the world. Gratitude enriches you with all the riches in life, because whatever you're grateful for multiplies!

The Key of Play

There is one certain way you can make yourself feel better about any subject in your life, and that is to create games with your imagination, and play. Play is fun, and so when you play, you feel really good.

At some point, we stopped playing and having fun like we did as children, with the result that as we became adults, we became more serious about life. But seriousness brings serious circumstances into your life. When you play and have fun, you feel really good, and – voilà – really good circumstances come into your life.

Life is supposed to be fun. Play with the law of attraction, invent games with your imagination, because the law of attraction doesn't know or care if you're imagining and playing, or if it is real. Whatever you give in imagination and feeling, will become real!

How to Play

> *"The law of love could be best understood*
> *and learned through little children."*

Mahatma Gandhi (1869-1948)
INDIAN POLITICAL LEADER

How do you play? You do the same thing as you did when you were a child, and you use your imagination to create make-believe games.

Let's imagine you're a cyclist and you want to become the best cyclist in the world and win the Tour de France. Your training is going well and you have your dream in your sights, but you are diagnosed with a disease and given a 40 percent chance to survive. While having treatment, you imagine you are riding in the Tour de France and it is the race of your life. You imagine the medical staff is your training team giving you feedback at every checkpoint. Each day you imagine you're racing in a time trial, and your time is getting better and better! You win the race with your medical team and you overcome the disease.

One year after you win back your health, you win the Tour de France, and you continue to win it seven years in a row, becoming the only cyclist in history to achieve that! This is what Lance Armstrong did. He used the most difficult

circumstances as props to create an imaginary game and
realize his dream.

Let's say you want to have the best-built body in the world,
and you also want to become a famous actor in America. You
live in a tiny village in Europe and come from a family that has
struggled financially, but still you imagine your dreams. You
use a picture of a hero to sculpt your body, and you imagine
winning the European title for the best-built body. You win
the title seven times, and then it is time to become a famous
actor. You travel to America, but no one believes you are actor
material, and they give you all the reasons why you will never
achieve your dream. But you have imagined being a famous
actor, and you can feel the success, you can taste it, and you
know it will happen. This is what Arnold Schwarzenegger did
when he won Mr. Olympia seven times and then became one
of the biggest names in Hollywood.

Imagine you want to be a great inventor. In your
childhood your mind is challenged to the extreme; you are
overwhelmed with hallucinations and blinding flashes of light.
You fail to finish university and leave your job due to a nervous
breakdown. To gain relief from the crippling hallucinations,
you take control of your mind by creating your own imaginary
world. Inspired by the idea of a brighter future, you direct
your imagination to new inventions. You build an invention
completely in your imagination; you change the construction,
make improvements, and even operate the device, without
ever drawing a sketch. You create a laboratory in your mind

and you use your imagination to check the new invention for
wear and tear, before turning your idea into a physical device.
This is what Nikola Tesla did to become one of the greatest
inventors. Whether it was the alternating current motor,
radio, amplifier, wireless communication, fluorescent light,
laser beam, remote control, or any of his other three hundred
plus patented inventions, all of them had been developed in
exactly this way – through the power of his imagination.

> *"Logic will get you from A to B. Imagination
> will take you everywhere."*
>
> *Albert Einstein* (1879-1955)
> NOBEL PRIZE–WINNING PHYSICIST

Whatever it is you want, use your imagination, create
games, and play. Use every prop you can find to help you.
If you want to lose weight or have a better body, then create
games so you feel as though you have that body now. You
can surround yourself with pictures of great bodies, but the
trick is this. You must imagine those bodies are *yours*! You
must imagine and feel that you are looking at *your* body, not
somebody else's body.

If you are overweight or underweight, and you had the
perfect weight right now, how would you feel? You would feel
different from how you feel now. Everything about you would
change. You would walk differently, talk differently, and you
would do things differently. Walk like that now! Talk like that

now! Act as if you have it now! It doesn't matter what it is that you want; imagine how you would feel with it, and act like that now in your imagination. Whatever you imagine with feeling, you are giving to the law of attraction, and you must receive it.

Lance Armstrong, Arnold Schwarzenegger, Nikola Tesla – all these people played with their imaginations and felt their dreams with all their heart. Their imaginings became so real to them, they could *feel* their dreams and know they would happen. It doesn't matter how far away your dream seems to you. It is closer to you than anything in your life, because all the power to bring your dream to you is inside you!

> *"Everything is possible for the person who believes."*
>
> *Jesus* (CIRCA 5 BC–CIRCA AD 30)
> FOUNDER OF CHRISTIANITY, IN MARK 9:23

In the future we will see more and more discoveries about the power of our imagination. Already scientists have discovered special mirror cells that activate the same areas in the brain when you imagine doing something as when you physically perform the action. In other words, simply by your playing and imagining what you want to experience, your brain immediately responds as if it is real.

If you're talking about something in the past or the future, you're imagining those things now, you're feeling those things now, you're on that frequency now, and that's what the law of attraction is receiving. When you're imagining your dream, the law of attraction is receiving it now. Remember, there is no time for the law of attraction. There is only this moment of now.

If you experience a time delay in receiving what you want, it's only because of the time it takes *you* to get onto the same feeling frequency that your desire is on. And to get onto the same frequency as your desire, you have to feel the love of having your desire now! When you get yourself onto the same feeling frequency and stay there, what you desire appears.

> *"All you can possibly need or desire is already yours. Call your desires into being by imagining and feeling your wish fulfilled."*
>
> *Neville Goddard* (1905-1972)
> NEW THOUGHT AUTHOR

When you are really excited about anything that has happened, and you feel amazing, capture that energy and imagine your dream. Quick flashes of imagining and feeling your dream are all you need to harness the power of your excited feelings for what you want! This is playing. This is fun. This is the joy of creating your life.

POINTS OF POWER

The Key of Love

- *To use love as the ultimate power in your life, you must love like you have never loved before. Fall in love with life!*

- *See only love, hear only love, speak only love, and feel love with all your heart.*

- *There is no limit, no ceiling, to the amount of love you can feel, and it is all inside you! You are made of love.*

- *Tell the law of attraction what you love every day by singling out the things you love and feeling them.*

- *To change the way you feel, or to lift good feelings higher, make a mental list of everything you love and adore!*

- *Your job is to love as much as possible every day.*

- *Make a conscientious effort to notice as many things around you that you love, as much as you can each day.*

The Key of Gratitude

- *Every time you feel grateful you are giving love.*

- *Be grateful for everything you have received in your life (past).
  Be grateful for everything you are receiving in your life (present).
  Be grateful for what you want in your life, as though you have
  received it (future).*

- *Your gratitude will multiply everything in your life.*

- *Gratitude is the bridge from negative feelings to harnessing
  the force of love!*

- *To use the power of gratitude, practice it. When anything good
  happens to you in your day, give thanks. It doesn't matter how
  small it is, say thank you.*

- *The more you feel gratitude, the more love you give; and the
  more love you give, the more you receive.*

- *Every spare second is an opportunity to be grateful and multiply
  the things you love.*

The Key of Play

- *When you play you feel really good – and really good circumstances come into your life. Seriousness brings serious circumstances.*

- *Life is supposed to be fun!*

- *The law of attraction doesn't know if you're imagining and playing, so whatever you give in imagination and play will become real!*

- *Whatever it is you want, use your imagination, use every prop you can find, create games, and play.*

- *Act as if you have it now! Whatever you imagine with feeling, you are giving to the law of attraction, and you must receive it.*

- *If you experience a delay in receiving what you want, it's only because of the time it takes you to get onto the same feeling frequency as your desire.*

- *When you are excited about anything and you feel amazing, capture that energy and imagine your dream.*

THE POWER
AND MONEY

"Poverty consists in feeling poor."

Ralph Waldo Emerson (1803-1882)

TRANSCENDENTALIST AUTHOR

How do you feel about money? Most people would say they love money, but if they don't have enough, they don't feel good about it at all. If a person has all the money they need, then most certainly they feel good about money. So you can tell how you feel about money, because if you don't have all you need, then you don't feel good about money.

If you look out into the world, you will see that the majority of people don't feel good about money, because the majority of the world's money and riches is in the hands of about 10 percent of the people. The only difference between the wealthy people and everyone else is that the wealthy people give more good feelings about money than they do bad feelings. It's as simple as that.

Why is it that so many people feel bad about money? It's not because they have never had money, because most of the people who have money began with nothing. The reason why so many people feel bad about money is that they have negative beliefs about money, and those negative beliefs were fed into their subconscious minds when they were children. Beliefs like "We can't afford that," "Money is evil," "Rich people must be dishonest," "Wanting money is wrong and it's not spiritual," "Having plenty of money means hard work."

When you're a child, you accept just about everything your parents, teachers, or society tell you. And so without realizing it, you grow up having negative feelings about money. The irony is that, at the same time that you're told that wanting money is wrong, you are told that you have to earn a living, even if it means doing work you don't love. Maybe you were even told that there are only certain jobs you can do to earn a living, that it's a limited list.

None of these things is true. The people who told you these things are innocent because they were passing on what they believed and felt was true, but because they believed it, the law of attraction made it true in their lives. Now you are learning that life works in a completely different way. If you lack money in your life, it is because you are giving out more bad feelings than you are giving good feelings about money.

> *"When you realize there is nothing lacking,*
> *the whole world belongs to you."*
>
> *Lao Tzu* (CIRCA 6TH CENTURY BC)
> FOUNDER OF TAOISM

Love Is Sticking Power

I came from a humble background, and even though my parents didn't want a lot of money, they struggled to make ends meet. So I grew up with the same negative beliefs about money as most people. I knew I had to change how I felt about money to change my circumstances, and I knew I had to change myself completely so money would not only come to me but stick to me!

I could see that the people who had money not only attracted it to themselves, but they also made money stick to themselves. If you took all the money in the world and you distributed it equally to every person, within a short time all the money would be back in the hands of the few percent, because the law of attraction must follow love, and so the few percent who feel good about money would magnetize it back to them. The force of love moves all the money and riches in the world, and it moves it according to law.

"This is an eternal and fundamental principle, inherent in all things, in every system of philosophy, in every religion, and in every science. There is no getting away from the law of love."

Charles Haanel (1866–1949)

NEW THOUGHT AUTHOR

You can see the law of attraction working when people win the lottery. They imagined and felt with all their heart that they would win the lottery. They spoke about *when* they win the lottery, not *if* they win the lottery, and they planned and imagined what they would do *when* they won. And they won! But the statistics on lottery winners show the real evidence of money sticking or not. Within a few years of winning the lottery, the majority of people have lost the money and are in more debt than before they won the lottery.

This happens because they used the law of attraction to win the lottery, but even when they received money, they didn't change how they really felt about money, and they lost it all. The money didn't stick to them!

When you don't feel good about money, you repel it. It will never stick to you. Even when you get some extra money you hadn't figured on receiving, in no time at all you will find that it has slipped through your fingers. Bigger bills come in, things break down, and unforeseen circumstances of every kind occur, all of which drains you of money and takes it right out of your hands.

So what is it that makes money stick? Love! Love is the attracting force that brings money, and love is also the power that makes money stick! It has nothing to do with whether you are a good person or not. That aspect of you is beyond any question whatsoever, because you are far more magnificent than you realize.

You have to give love and feel good about money to bring it to you and make it stick! Right now if you lack money, and your credit card debt is increasing, you have no sticking power and you are repelling money.

It doesn't matter what financial state you are in now. It doesn't matter what financial state your business, your country, or the world is in. There is no such thing as a hopeless situation. There are people who lived during the Great Depression who thrived because they knew the law of love and attraction. They lived the law by imagining and feeling everything they wanted, and they defied the circumstances that surrounded them.

"Let our lives be good, and the times are good. We make our times; such as we are, such are the times."

Saint Augustine of Hippo (354-430)
THEOLOGIAN AND BISHOP

The force of love can break through every single obstacle or situation. World problems are no obstacle for the force of love. The law of attraction operates with the same power whether the times are up or down.

How to Change the Way You Feel About Money

When you change the way you feel about money, the amount of money in your life will change. The better you feel about money, the more money you magnetize to yourself.

If you don't have much money, then receiving bills won't make you feel good. But the moment you react negatively to a big bill, you give bad feelings, and most surely you will receive bigger bills. Whatever you give, you receive back. The most important thing is that when you pay your bills, you find a way, any way, to make yourself feel good. Never pay your bills when you don't feel good, because you will just bring bigger bills to you.

To change what you're feeling, you need to use your imagination to turn your bills into something that makes you feel better. You can imagine they're not really bills at all but instead you've decided to donate money to each company or person out of the goodness of your heart, because of the wonderful service they provide.

Imagine your bills are checks you're receiving. Or use gratitude and give thanks to the company who sent you the bill, by thinking about how you've benefited from their service – for electricity or being able to live in a home. You can write across the front of a bill when you pay it, "Thank you – paid." If you don't have the money to pay the bill right away, write across the front of it, "Thank you for the money." The law of attraction doesn't question whether what you imagine and feel is real or not. It responds to what you give, period.

> *"You are rewarded not according to your work or your time but according to the measure of your love."*
>
> *Saint Catherine of Siena* (1347-1380)
> PHILOSOPHER AND DOCTOR OF THE CATHOLIC CHURCH

When you receive your salary, be grateful for it so it multiplies! Most people don't even feel good when they are paid, because they're so worried about how to make their salary last. They miss an incredible opportunity to give love every time they're paid. When some money comes into your hands, no matter how little it is, be grateful! Remember, whatever you're grateful for multiplies. Gratitude is the great multiplier!

Seize Every Opportunity to Play

Seize every moment that you are handling money to make the money multiply by feeling good. Feel love when you pay for anything! Feel love when you hand over money! Feel love with all your heart by imagining how much your money is helping the company and the staff who work for the company. It will make you feel good about the money you're giving instead of feeling bad because you have less money. The difference between the two is the difference between having plenty of money and struggling with money for the rest of your life.

Here is a game you can play so you remember to feel good about money each time you handle it. Imagine a dollar bill. Imagine the front of the dollar bill as the positive side, which represents plenty of money. Imagine the back of the dollar bill as the negative side representing a lack of money. Each time you handle money, deliberately flip the bills so the front is facing you. Put bills in your wallet with the front facing you. When you hand over money, make sure the front is facing upward. By doing this you are using money as your cue to remember to feel good about plenty of money.

If you are using a credit card, then flip the credit card to the front where your name is, because the front of your credit card is telling you that there is an abundance of money and it has your name on it!

When you pay for anything, as you hand over your card or money, imagine an abundance of money for the person you are handing it to, and mean it. Whatever you give out, you receive back!

Imagine that you are wealthy right now. Imagine that you have all the money you need right now. How would you live your life differently? Think about all the things you would do. How would you feel? You would feel different and because you would feel different, you would walk differently. You would talk differently. You would hold your body in a different way, and you would move differently. You would react differently to everything. Your reaction to bills would be different. Your reaction to people, circumstances, events, and everything in life would be different. Because you would *feel* different! You would be relaxed. You would have peace of mind. You would feel happy. You would be easygoing about everything. You would enjoy every day, without giving any thought to tomorrow. That's the feeling you want to capture. That is the feeling of love for money, and that feeling is magnetically sticky!

"Capture the feeling associated with your realized wish by assuming the feeling that would be yours were you already in possession of the thing you desire, and your wish will objectify itself."

Neville Goddard (1905-1972)
NEW THOUGHT AUTHOR

Say Yes to Money

Remember, any time you hear of another person receiving more money or success, get excited, because it means you're on that frequency! It is evidence that you're on a good frequency, so be as excited as if it were happening to you, because your reaction to the news is everything. If you react with joy and excitement for the other person, you are saying *yes* to more money and success for yourself. If you react by feeling disappointed or envious that it's not happening to you, your bad feelings are saying *no* to more money and success for yourself. If you hear of a person winning the lottery, or you hear of a company making record profits, be excited and happy for them. The fact that you heard the news tells you that you're on the same frequency, and your reaction of feeling good feelings for those people says *yes* for you!

A few years ago, I reached an all-time low with money in my life. I had several credit cards that I had charged up, my apartment was mortgaged to the limit, and my company was in debt for millions of dollars because I was making a film called *The Secret*. I think my situation with money was about as bad as anybody's can get. I wanted money to finish the film, I knew the law of attraction, and I knew I had to feel good about money to bring it to me. But it wasn't easy because every single day I was confronted by the mounting debt, with people calling for money, and had no idea how I would be able to pay my staff's wages. So I took drastic action.

I walked to an ATM and drew out several hundred dollars from my credit card account. I needed that money so badly to pay bills and buy food, but I took the money in my hand, walked down a busy street, and I gave the money away to people on the street.

I put a $50 bill in my hand, and as I walked, I looked at each person's face as they walked toward me, trying to decide who to give the money to. I wanted to give money to every single person, but I only had a certain amount. I let my heart choose and I gave the money away to all kinds of people. It was the first time in my life I had felt love for money. But it wasn't the money itself that caused me to feel love, it was giving the money to people that made me feel love for money. It was a Friday, and afterward I had tears of joy all weekend about how good it felt to give money.

On Monday afternoon something astounding happened: my bank account received $25,000 through the most incredible sequence of events. That $25,000 literally fell out of the sky into my life and into my account. I had bought some shares in a friend's company years earlier, and I had forgotten about them because they had never increased in value. But that Monday morning I received a phone call asking me if I would sell my shares as they had skyrocketed in value, and by Monday afternoon the money for the shares was in my account.

I didn't set out to give money away to bring more money to me. I gave it away so I would feel love about money. I wanted to change a lifetime of feeling bad about money. If I had given away that money in order to get money, it would never have worked, because it would have meant I was motivated by feeling a lack of money, which is negative, instead of being motivated by love. But if you give money away, and if you feel love when you give it, most surely it will return to you. One man wrote a check and donated $100 to a charity he felt was really worthwhile. Within ten hours of writing the check, he closed the largest sale he had ever had in his company.

> *"It's not how much we give but how much love
> we put into giving."*
>
> *Mother Teresa* (1910-1997)
> NOBEL PEACE PRIZE–WINNING MISSIONARY

If you are struggling with money, in order to feel really good about money, you can send thoughts of abundance of money to the people whom you pass on the street during the day. Look at each of their faces and imagine giving them plenty of money, and imagine their joy. Feel it, and move on to the next person. It's a simple thing to do, but if you really feel it, it will change how you feel about money, and it will change the circumstances of money in your life.

Career and Business

> *"True genius without heart is a thing of naught – for not great understanding alone, not intelligence alone, nor both together make genius. Love! Love! Love! That is the soul of genius."*

Nikolaus Joseph von Jacquin (1727-1817)
DUTCH SCIENTIST

It's the attractive force of love that moves all the money in the world, and whoever is giving love by feeling good is a magnet for money. You don't have to earn money to prove yourself. You are worthy of all the money you need now! You are deserving of the money you need now! You are meant to work for the joy of it. You're meant to work because it thrills and excites you. You're meant to work because you love it! And when you love what you do, money follows!

If you're doing a job because you believe it's the only way you can earn money, and you don't love it, you'll never bring money or the job you love that way. The job you love exists now, and all you have to do to bring it to you is give love. Imagine and feel having the job now and you will receive it. Look for everything that's good about the job you have and love those things, because when you give love, everything you love follows. The job you love will walk right into your life!

An unemployed man applied for a job he had always wanted. After applying for the job, he created a pretend offer letter from the company that included his salary and details of his job. He created a business card with his name and the company's logo, and he looked at the card with feelings of gratitude that he worked for the company. He wrote congratulatory emails to himself every few days for getting the job.

This man progressed through the phone interview, to face-to-face interviews with ten people. Two hours after his interviews, the company called with the news that he had the job. This man received the job he had always wanted with a far greater salary than he had written in his imaginary offer letter.

Even if you don't know what you want to do in your life, all you have to do is give love through good feelings, and you will magnetize everything you love to yourself. Your feelings of love will lead you to your purpose. Your dream job is on the frequency of love and to receive it, you just have to get yourself there.

"Success is not the key to happiness. Happiness is the key to success."

Albert Schweitzer (1875-1965)
NOBEL PEACE PRIZE–WINNING
MEDICAL MISSIONARY AND PHILOSOPHER

Success in business operates in exactly the same way. If you have a business but it's not doing as well as you want, then something isn't sticky about your business. The biggest thing that causes businesses to become unstuck is giving bad feelings about the lack of success. Even if the business has been going well, if you react with bad feelings when there's a slight dip, you will create a bigger downturn in your business. All the inspirations and ideas that will make your business skyrocket to levels you can scarcely imagine are on the frequency of love, so you have to find ways to feel good about your business and get yourself onto the highest frequency you can.

Imagine, play, and create games, and do whatever you can to lift your spirits and feel good. When you lift your feelings, you will lift your business. In every part of your life, every day, love everything you see, love everything around you, and love the success of other companies as though it were your success! If you feel really good about success, no matter whose success it is, you stick success to you!

In business or whatever job or work you do, make sure that you *give* in equal value to the money you *receive* in profits or from your salary. If you give less value than the money you receive, your business or your career will be doomed to failure. You simply can't take from anyone in life, because you will take from yourself. At all times give equal value for what you're receiving. The only way you can be sure of doing that is to give *more* value than the money you're receiving. If you give more value than the money you're receiving, your business and career will take off.

Love Has Unlimited Ways for You to Receive

Money is only a tool for you to experience the things you love in life. When you think about the things you can do with money, you will feel much more love and joy than when you think only of money. Imagine being with what you love, doing what you love, and having the things you love, because you will then feel far more love than you will if you only think about money.

The attractive force of love has unlimited ways for you to receive what you want, and only one of those ways involves money. Don't make the mistake of thinking that money is the only way you can receive something. That is limited thinking and you will limit your life!

My sister attracted a new car through the most adventurous sequence of events. She was driving to work and she got caught in a flash flood and her car stopped in the water. At the insistence of an emergency rescue worker she was carried to dry land, even though the water was not dangerously high. She laughed her way through the whole experience, and her rescue even made the nightly television news. My sister's car was irreparably damaged by the water, and within two weeks she was given a large check, and she bought her dream car.

The most wonderful part of this story is that my sister was renovating a house at the time, and she didn't have any spare money for a new car. She didn't even imagine having a new car. She had attracted the beautiful new car to her because she had cried tears of joy when she heard the news that our other sibling had gotten a new car. My sister was so happy and gave so much love for our sibling receiving a new car that the law of attraction moved every element, circumstance, and event to deliver a new car to her too. That is the power of love!

You will not know how you will receive what you want until you receive it, but the force of love knows. Get out of your own way, and have faith. Imagine what you want, feel the happiness inside you, and the attractive force of love will find the perfect way for you to receive it. Our human minds are limited but the intelligence of love is unlimited. Its ways are beyond our comprehension. Don't limit your life by thinking money is the only way to get something you want. Don't make money your only target, but make your target what you want to be, do, or have. If you want a new home, imagine and feel the joy of living in it. If you want beautiful clothes, appliances, or a car; if you want to go to college, move to another country, receive training in music, acting, or a sport – imagine it! All these things can come to you in an unlimited number of ways.

Love Rules

There is one rule with money: you can never put money ahead of love. If you do, you violate love's law of attraction, and you will suffer the consequences. Love must be the ruling force in your life. Nothing can ever be put above love. Money is a tool for you to use, and you bring it to yourself through love, but if you put money ahead of love in your life, it will cause you to receive a whole bunch of negative things. You can't give love for money and then walk around being rude and negative to people, because if you do that, you open the door for negativity to walk into your relationships, health, happiness, and finances.

*"If you require love, try to realize that the only
way to get love is by giving it, that the more you
give the more you will get, and the only way you
can give it is to fill yourself up with it, until you
become a magnet."*

Charles Haanel (1866-1949)

NEW THOUGHT AUTHOR

You are meant to have the money you need to live a full
life. You are not meant to be suffering from a lack of money,
because suffering adds negativity to the world. The beauty of
life is that when you put love first, all the money you need to
live a full life comes to you.

POINTS OF POWER

- *It's the attractive force of love that moves all the money in the world, and whoever is giving love by feeling good is a magnet for money.*

- *You can tell how you feel about money, because if you don't have all you need, then you don't feel good about money.*

- *Love is the attracting force that brings money, and love is also the power that makes money stick!*

- *When you pay your bills, find a way, any way, to make yourself feel good. Imagine your bills are checks you're receiving. Or use gratitude and give thanks to the company who sent you the bill.*

- *When some money comes into your hands, no matter how small it is, be grateful! Remember, gratitude is the great multiplier.*

- *Feel love when you pay for anything instead of feeling bad because you have less money. The difference between the two is the difference between having plenty of money, and struggling with money for the rest of your life.*

- *Use physical money as your cue to remember to feel good about plenty of money. Imagine the front of each bill as the positive side, which represents plenty of money. Each time you handle money, deliberately flip the bill so the front is facing you.*

- *If you feel really good about success, no matter whose success it is, you stick success to you!*

- *Give in equal value to the money you receive through profits or your salary. If you give more value than the money you're receiving, your business and career will take off.*

- *Money is only a tool for you to experience the things you love in life. The attractive force of love has unlimited ways for you to receive what you want, and only one of those ways involves money.*

- *Imagine being with what you love, doing what you love, and having the things you love, because you will feel far more love than you will if you only think about money.*

- *The beauty of life is that when you put love first, all the money you need to live a full life comes to you.*

THE POWER AND
RELATIONSHIPS

"Extend to each person, no matter how trivial the contact, all the care and kindness and understanding and love that you can muster, and do it with no thought of any reward. Your life will never be the same again."

Og Mandino (1923-1996)

AUTHOR

Giving love is the law that applies to everything in your life. And giving love is the law of relationships. The force of love doesn't care whether you know someone or not, whether a person is a friend or foe, a loved one or a complete stranger. The force of love doesn't care if you're encountering a work colleague, boss, parent, child, student, or a person serving you in a store. With every single person you come into contact with, you are either giving love or you're not. And what you give is what you will receive.

Relationships are your biggest channel to give love, and so you can change your entire life just through the love you give in your relationships. At the same time though, relationships can be your biggest downfall, because they are often your biggest excuse for *not* giving love!

What You Give to Others, You Give to Yourself

The most enlightened beings throughout history told us to love others. You were not told to love others just so that you would be a nice person. You were being given the secret to life! You were being given the law of attraction! When you love others, *you* will have an amazing life. When you love others, *you* will receive the life you deserve.

> *"The entire law is summed up in a single command, Love your neighbor as yourself."*
>
> *Saint Paul* (CIRCA 5-67)
> CHRISTIAN APOSTLE, IN GALATIANS 5:14

Give love to others through kindness, encouragement, support, gratitude, or any good feeling, and it comes back to you and multiplies itself, bringing love to every other area of your life, including your health, money, happiness, and career.

Give negativity to others, through criticism, anger, impatience, or any bad feeling, and you will receive that negativity back – guaranteed! And as the negativity comes back, it multiplies itself, attracting more negativity, which affects the rest of your life.

It's Not About the Other Person

You can tell in your relationships right now what you've been giving. If a current relationship is great, it means you are giving more love and gratitude than negativity. If a current relationship is difficult or challenging, it means you are inadvertently giving more negativity than love.

Some people think a relationship is either good or bad because of the other person, but life doesn't happen that way. You can't say to the force of love, "I will give love only when the other person gives it to me!" You can't receive anything in life unless you give it first! Whatever you give, you receive, so it's not about the other person at all: it's all about you! It's all about what you are giving and what you are feeling.

You can change any relationship right now by looking for the things you love, appreciate, and are grateful for in that person. When you make a deliberate effort to look for the things you love more than you notice negative things, a miracle will take place. It will appear to you as though something incredible has happened to the other person. But it's the force of love that is incredible, because it dissolves negativity, including negativity in relationships. All you have to do is harness the force of love by looking for the things you love in the person, and everything will change in the relationship!

I know of hundreds of relationships that have been restored through the power of love, but one particular story of a woman who used love's power to restore her crumbling marriage stands out from the others, because this woman had lost all love for her husband. In fact, she couldn't bear to be near him. Her husband complained every day. He was sick all the time. He was depressed and angry, and verbally abusive to her and their four children.

When the woman learned about the power of giving love, she decided right away to feel happier despite the problems in her marriage. Immediately the atmosphere in their home became lighter, and the woman's relationships with her children got better. She then went through her photo albums, looking at the photos of her husband when they first married. She took some of the photos and put them on her desk to look at them every day, and by her doing this, something amazing happened. She felt the love she had first felt for her husband, and as she felt the love return, her feelings of love began to increase dramatically inside her. She reached a point where she loved her husband more than she ever had in her life. Her love became so great that her husband's depression and anger disappeared, and his health began to return. This woman went from wanting to be as far away as possible from her husband to a marriage where they want to be with each other as much as possible.

Love Means Freedom

Now here is the tricky bit with giving love in relationships, and it's the one thing that has prevented many from receiving the life they deserve. It's only tricky because people have misunderstood what it means to give love to others. To be very clear about what it means to give love to others, you need to understand what it means *not* to give love to others.

Trying to change another person is *not* giving love! Thinking you know what is best for another person is *not* giving love! Thinking you are right and another person is wrong is *not* giving love! Criticizing, blaming, complaining, nagging, or finding fault with another person is *not* giving love!

> *"Hate is not conquered by hate. Hate is conquered by love. This is a law eternal."*
>
> *Gautama Buddha* (563-483 BC)
> FOUNDER OF BUDDHISM

I want to share a story I received that demonstrates the care we must take in our relationships. A man's wife had left him and had taken their children with her. The man was devastated, he blamed his wife, and he refused to accept her decision. He continued to contact her, determined to do everything he could to change her mind. He may have thought he was acting out of love for his wife and family, but his actions were not loving. He blamed his wife for their marriage ending. He believed that she was wrong and he was right. He refused to accept his wife's decision to choose for herself. Because he would not stop contacting his wife, he was arrested and sentenced to jail.

The man eventually realized that he was not giving love when he denied his wife *her* freedom to choose what she wanted, and that he lost *his* freedom as a result. The law of attraction is the law of love and you cannot break it. If you violate it, you break yourself.

I am sharing this story because the ending of intimate relationships is very challenging for some people. You cannot deny someone else's right to choose what they want, because that is not giving love. It is a bitter pill to swallow when your heart is breaking, but you must respect everyone's freedom and right to choose. What you give to another person you receive yourself, and when you deny another person's freedom to choose, you will attract negative things that deny your own freedom. Maybe the flow of money to you decreases, or your health weakens, or your job takes a downturn, because all of these things would affect your freedom. There is no "other person" for the law of attraction. What you give out to others, you give to yourself.

Giving love to other people does not mean you let people walk all over you or abuse you in any way, because that's not giving love either. Allowing another person to use you doesn't help that person, and it surely doesn't help you. Love is tough, and we learn and grow through its law, and as part of that learning we experience consequences. So it is not love to allow another person to use or abuse you. The answer is, get yourself onto the highest frequency of good feelings that you can, and the force of love will resolve the situation *for* you.

> *"Whenever anyone has offended me, I try to raise my soul so high that the offense cannot reach it."*
>
> René Descartes (1596-1650)
>
> MATHEMATICIAN AND PHILOSOPHER

The Secret to Relationships

Life presents everything to you so that you can choose what you love. And part of the gift of life is that you are given all kinds of people, so you can choose what you love in those people and turn away from what you don't love. You are not meant to manufacture love for qualities in a person you don't love, but simply to turn away without giving them any feeling.

Turning away from what you don't love in someone means you're relaxed about it, and you know life is giving you a choice. It doesn't mean that you argue with them to prove they're wrong or you criticize or blame them, or that you want to change them because you think you're right. Because if you do any of these things, you are not giving love – big time!

"Your own soul is nourished when you are kind;
it is destroyed when you are cruel."

King Solomon (CIRCA IOTH CENTURY BC)
BIBLICAL KING OF ISRAEL, IN PROVERBS 11:17

When you are on a feeling frequency of love, then only people who are on the same feeling frequency as you are can come into your life.

You know some days you feel really happy, some days you feel irritated, and others you feel sad. You can be many different versions of yourself. A person in a relationship with you can also be many versions, including happy, irritated, or sad. No doubt you will have seen them being many different versions, but every version is still that person. When you're happy, then only the happy version of other people can come into your life. But *you* have to be happy to receive the happy versions of other people!

It doesn't mean you are responsible for other people's happiness, because everyone is responsible for their own lives and happiness. What it means is there's nothing else for you to do but to feel happy yourself, and the law of attraction will do the rest.

"Happiness depends upon ourselves."

Aristotle (384-322 BC)

GREEK PHILOSOPHER AND SCIENTIST

PETs

One way to take the sting out of confrontational or difficult relationships is to imagine people as your own "Personal Emotional Trainers"! The force of love presents you with a whole array of Personal Emotional Trainers, disguised as everyday people, but they are all training you to choose love!

Some people may be soft Personal Emotional Trainers because they don't push you very hard and they're so easy to love. Some people may be tough Personal Emotional Trainers because they push you to your limits, as some personal physical trainers do, but they are the ones who are making you stronger to choose love no matter what.

Personal Emotional Trainers can use all kinds of situations and tactics to challenge you, but the thing to remember is that every challenge is presented so you will choose love and turn away from negativity and blame. Some trainers may challenge you to judge them or others, but don't fall for that trap. Judgment is negative and it's not giving love, so if you can't love the good in someone or something, simply turn away.

Some trainers may test you by provoking you to feel revenge, anger, or hatred. Turn away by looking for the things you love in life. Some trainers may even hit you with guilt, feelings of unworthiness, or fear. Don't fall for any of them, because negativity of any kind is not love.

> *"Hatred paralyzes life; love releases it.*
> *Hatred confuses life; love harmonizes it.*
> *Hatred darkens life; love illuminates it."*
>
> *Martin Luther King Jr.* (1929-1968)
> BAPTIST MINISTER AND CIVIL RIGHTS LEADER

If you imagine the people in your life as your Personal Emotional Trainers, it will help you with any difficult relationships. It's the tough trainers who make you stronger and determined to choose love no matter what, but they're also giving you a message. They're telling you that you've gotten yourself onto a negative feeling frequency – and you need to feel better to move off it! No one can come into your life and affect you negatively, unless you are already on the same negative feeling frequency. If you're on a feeling frequency of love, it won't matter how tough or negative someone is, they will not and cannot affect you!

Each person is just doing their job, just as you are doing your job of being a Personal Emotional Trainer to others. There are no enemies, there are only some great PETs, and some tough PETs who are making you great.

The Law of Attraction Is a Sticky Business

The law of attraction is a sticky business. When you rejoice in another person's good fortune, their good fortune sticks to you! When you admire or appreciate anything about another person, you're sticking those qualities to yourself. But when you think or discuss negative things about someone else, you're sticking those negative things to you too, and you're putting them into your own life.

The law of attraction is responding to *your* feelings. Whatever you give, you receive, and so if you stick a label on any person, circumstance, or event in life, you are sticking the label on you, and that's what you will receive.

Now this is fantastic news, because it means you can stick everything you love and want to you by looking for the things you love in other people, and saying yes to them with all of your heart! The world is your catalogue, and when you understand the power of your love, it is a full-time job noticing everything you love in other people. But it's the easiest and best way to change your whole life. It beats struggle and suffering. All you have to do is notice the things you love in other people, and turn away from the things you don't so you don't give them any feeling. How easy is that?

"Taking the first footstep with a good thought, the second with a good word, and the third with a good deed, I entered Paradise."

Book of Arda Viraf (CIRCA 6TH CENTURY)
ZOROASTRIAN RELIGIOUS TEXT

Gossip Is Sticky Too

Gossip seems harmless on the surface, but it can cause a lot of negative things in people's lives. Gossip is not giving love. Gossip is giving negativity and that's exactly what you receive back. Gossip is not harmful to the person who is being spoken of; gossip harms those gossiping!

When you are talking with a family member or a friend, and they tell you about some negative thing that someone said or did they are gossiping and they are giving out negativity. As you listen to them, you are giving out negativity too because you are a feeling being, and you can't hear negative things without your feelings dropping rapidly. When you talk with a work colleague at lunch, and you both talk negatively about someone, you are gossiping and you are giving out negativity. You can't talk about or hear negativity and have good feelings!

So to put it frankly, we need to be mindful of not sticking our nose in other people's business, because their business will get stuck on our nose! Unless you want it in your life, turn away from it without feeling anything. You'll not only be doing yourself a favor, but you'll also be doing the other people a favor who don't realize the negative effect gossip can have on their lives.

If you find yourself gossiping or listening to gossip, stop midsentence and say, "But I am so grateful that . . ." and finish the sentence with something good about the person being gossiped about.

> *"If a man speaks or acts with an evil thought, pain follows him. If a man speaks or acts with a pure thought, happiness follows him, like a shadow that never leaves him."*
>
> *Gautama Buddha* (563-483 BC)
> FOUNDER OF BUDDHISM

Your Reaction Chooses It

Life is presenting every person and circumstance to you so you can choose what you love and what you don't love. When you react to anything, you are reacting with your feelings, and as you do, you are choosing it! Your reaction, whether good or bad, sticks it to you, and in effect, you are saying you want more of it! And so it's important to watch how you react in your relationships, because whether you react with good or bad feelings, they're the feelings you're giving, and you will receive more of the same circumstances to make you feel that way.

If a person says or does something, and you find yourself feeling upset, offended, or angry, do your best to change the negative reaction right away. Simply being aware that you've reacted negatively takes the power out of the negative feelings immediately and can even stop them. But if you feel as though the negative feelings have a grip on you, it is best to walk away and spend a couple of minutes looking for the things you love, one after the other until you feel much better. You can use anything you love to make you feel better, like listening to your favorite music, imagining the things you love, or doing something you love. You can also think about the things you love in the person who upset you. This might be challenging, but if you can do it, it is the fastest way to feel better. It's also the fastest way to become the master of your feelings!

> *"A man who is master of himself can end a sorrow*
> *as he can invent a pleasure. I don't want to be*
> *at the mercy of my emotions. I want to use them,*
> *to enjoy them, and to dominate them."*
>
> Oscar *Wilde* (1854–1900)
> AUTHOR AND POET

You can change any negative situation in your life, but you can't change it with bad feelings. You have to react differently to the situation because if you keep reacting negatively, your bad feelings will magnify and multiply the negativity. When you give good feelings, the positivity magnifies, and multiplies. Even if you can't imagine how a particular situation can change into something positive – it can! The force of love always finds a way.

Love Is a Shield

To take the power out of other people's negativity and not be affected by it, remember the magnetic fields of feelings surrounding each person. There's a field of love, joy, happiness, gratitude, excitement, passion, and a field for every good feeling. There's also a field of anger, discouragement, frustration, hate, desire for revenge, fear, and a field for every negative feeling.

A person surrounded by a magnetic field of anger doesn't feel good at all, and so if you come into their presence, they will most likely direct their anger at you. They don't mean to harm you, but they can't see anything good when they're looking at the world through their field of anger. All they can see are things that anger them. And because they can only see anger, they are likely to get angry and hurl anger at the first person they see – often a loved one. Does this situation sound familiar?

If you're feeling fantastic, the force of your magnetic field creates a shield that no negativity can penetrate. And so it won't matter what negativity anyone hurls at you, it cannot touch you, and it will bounce right off your feeling field without affecting you at all.

On the other hand, if a person hurls something negative at you and you feel what they say, then you know that your feelings must have dropped, because the negativity broke through your feeling field. There's only one thing to do if this happens, and that is to find an excuse to politely walk away, so you can restore yourself with good feelings. Two negative fields multiply at a rapid rate when they come into contact with each other, and no good can ever come of it. You will know this from your own life experience; two negative fields together are not a pretty sight!

"Muddy water, let stand, becomes clear."

Lao Tzu (CIRCA 6TH CENTURY BC)

FOUNDER OF TAOISM

If you are feeling sad, disappointed, frustrated, or any negative feeling, then you are looking at the world through that feeling field, and the world will look sad, disappointing, or frustrating to you. You cannot see anything good through a field of bad feelings. Not only is your negative field attracting more negativity to itself, but you will never see your way out of any problem until you change the way you feel. Changing

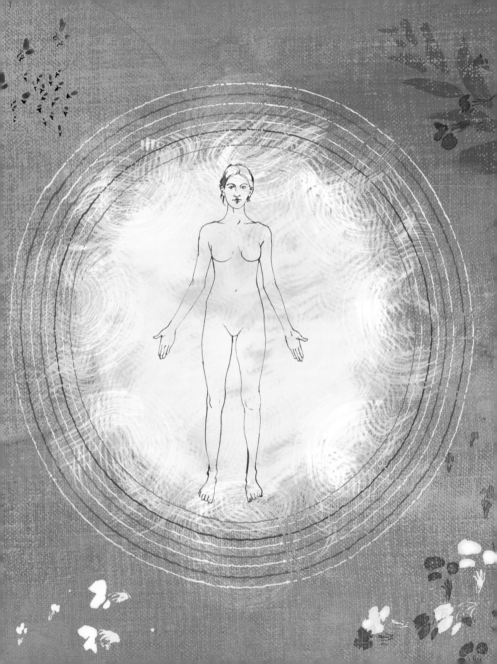

the way you feel is easy compared to running around trying to change the circumstances of the outside world. All the physical action in the world cannot change the situation. Change your feelings and the outside circumstances will change!

> *"The power is from within, but we cannot receive it unless we give it."*
>
> *Charles Haanel* (1866-1949)
> NEW THOUGHT AUTHOR

When someone is surrounded by a magnetic field of joy, you can feel their joy touch you from across the room. People who are popular and who have magnetic personalities are simply people who feel good most of the time. The field of joy that surrounds them is so magnetic that it draws everybody and everything to them.

The more you give love and feel good, the more magnetic your field becomes and the more it expands, drawing everything and everyone you love to you! Imagine that!

Love Is the Power That Connects Everything

*"When all the people in the world love one another,
then the strong will not overpower the weak, the
many will not oppress the few, the wealthy will
not mock the poor, the honored will not disdain the
humble, and the cunning will not deceive the simple."*

Mozi (CIRCA 470-CIRCA 391 BC)

CHINESE PHILOSOPHER

You have opportunities every day to give love to other
people through your good feelings. When you feel happy, it
is your guarantee that you will be giving positivity and love
to whomever you come into contact with. When you give love
to anyone, the love will return to you, but in a far greater way
than you may have realized.

When you give love to another person, if your love affects
the other person so positively that they then give love to
someone else, then no matter how many people are positively
affected, no matter how far your love travels, *all* that love
comes back to *you*. Not only do you receive back the love
you gave to the original person, you receive all the love back
from everyone who was affected! And the love returns to
you dressed as positive circumstances, positive people, and
positive events in your life.

On the other hand, if you *negatively* affect another person so much that the person goes on to negatively affect someone else, then the negativity will return to you in full. You will receive it back in the form of negative circumstances affecting money, your career, your health, or your relationships. Whatever you give to another, you give to yourself.

"If you are distressed by anything external, the pain is not due to the thing itself, but to your estimate of it; and this you have the power to revoke at any moment."

Marcus Aurelius (121–180)
ROMAN EMPEROR

When you are feeling enthusiastic, happy, and cheerful, those good feelings affect everyone you come into contact with. Even if you connect with a person just briefly in a store, on a bus, or in an elevator, when your good feelings make a difference to any person you connect with, the affect of that one instance on *your* life is almost incomprehensible.

> *"Remember there's no such thing as a small act of kindness. Every act creates a ripple with no logical end."*
>
> *Scott Adams* (B. 1957)
> CARTOONIST

Love is the solution and the answer to every relationship. You can never improve a relationship with negativity. Use the Creation Process for your relationships, and give love to receive. Use the Keys to Power for your relationships. Notice the things you love, make lists of the things you love, talk about the things you love, and turn away from the things you don't love. Imagine having the perfect relationship, imagine it at the highest level you can, and feel having it with all your heart. If you find it difficult to feel good about a relationship, then love everything else around you, and just stop noticing the negative things in the relationship!

Love can do anything for you! All you have to do is give love by feeling good, and any negativity in your relationships will fade away. Whenever you are faced with a negative situation in a relationship, the solution is always love! You won't know *how* it will be solved, and you can never know how, but if you maintain feeling good and give love, it will happen.

The message from Lao Tzu, Buddha, Jesus, Muhammad, and every great being is loud and clear – love!

POINTS OF POWER

- *With every single person you come into contact, you are either giving love or you're not. And based on what you give, that is what you receive.*

- *Give love to others through kindness, encouragement, support, gratitude, or any good feeling, and it comes back to you multiplied in every area of your life.*

- *Look for the things you love in a relationship more than you notice negative things and it will appear as if something incredible has happened to the other person.*

- *Trying to change another person, thinking you know what is best for another person, thinking you are right and another person is wrong is not giving love!*

- *Criticizing, blaming, complaining, nagging, or finding fault with another person is not giving love!*

- *You have to be happy to receive the happy versions of other people!*

- *The force of love presents you with a whole array of Personal Emotional Trainers, disguised as everyday people, but they are all training you to choose love!*

- *You can stick everything you love and want to you by looking for the things you love in other people, and saying yes to those qualities with all of your heart!*

- *You can't talk about or hear negativity and have good feelings!*

- *Life is presenting every person and circumstance to you so you can choose what you love and what you don't love. When you react to anything, you are reacting with your feelings, and as you do, you are choosing it!*

- *You can't change a negative situation with bad feelings. If you keep reacting negatively, your bad feelings will magnify and multiply the negativity.*

- *If you're feeling fantastic, the force of your magnetic field creates a shield that no negativity can penetrate.*

- *Changing the way you feel is easy compared to running around trying to change the circumstances of the outside world. Change your feelings and the outside circumstances will change!*

- *The more you give love and feel good, the more magnetic your field becomes and the more it expands, drawing everything and everyone you love to you!*

THE POWER
AND HEALTH

"Natural forces within us are the true healers of disease."

Hippocrates (CIRCA 460 BC–CIRCA 370 BC)

FATHER OF WESTERN MEDICINE

What does it mean to be healthy? You may think that being healthy means that you are not sick, but being healthy is far more than that. If you feel okay, or average, or nothing much at all, you are not healthy.

Being healthy is feeling the same way as little children feel. Little children are bursting with energy every day. Their bodies feel light and flexible; moving is effortless. They're light on their feet. Their minds are clear; they're happy, and free of worry and stress. They sleep deeply and peacefully every night, and they wake up feeling completely refreshed, as if with a brand-new body. They feel passionate and excited about every new day. Look at little children and you will see what being healthy really means. It is the way you used to feel, and it is the way you should *still* feel!

You can feel this way most of the time, because unlimited health is available to you unceasingly through the force of love! There is never a second that anything is withheld from you. Whatever you want is yours, and that includes unlimited health. But you have to open the door to receive it!

What Do You Believe?

"For as he thinketh in his heart, so is he."

King Solomon (CIRCA 10TH CENTURY BC)
BIBLICAL KING OF ISRAEL, IN PROVERBS 23:7

These are among the greatest words of wisdom ever given, but what do they mean, "For as he thinketh in his heart, so is he"?

What you think in your heart is what you believe to be true. Beliefs are simply repeated thoughts with strong feelings attached to them like, "I catch colds easily," "I have a sensitive stomach," "I find it hard to lose weight," "I'm allergic to that," "Coffee keeps me awake." All these are beliefs, not facts. A belief is when you have made up your mind, the verdict is in, you've nailed the door shut and thrown away the key, and there is no room for negotiation. But whatever you believe and feel is true *will* be true for you, whether your beliefs help you or harm you. Whatever beliefs you give out, the law of attraction says you must receive back.

Many people have more fearful beliefs about disease than they have good beliefs about health. It's not surprising because of the attention that is given to disease in the world, and you are surrounded by that every day. In spite of all the advances in medicine, disease is increasing because people have become increasingly fearful of disease.

Do you have more good feelings about health than you have negative feelings about disease? Do you believe in lifelong health more than you believe in the inevitability of disease? If you believe that your body will deteriorate with age and that disease is inevitable, you are giving out that belief, and the law of attraction must return it to you clothed as the circumstances and state of your health and body.

"For the thing that I fear comes upon me, and what I dread befalls me."

Job 3:25

The placebo effect in medicine is proof of the power of belief. One group of patients is given real pills or treatment, and another group is given the placebo – a sugar pill or fake treatment – but neither is told which one is a cure for their symptoms or illness. Yet the group that gets the placebo often experiences significant improvements and the reduction or disappearance of symptoms. The startling results of the placebo effect regularly demonstrate the power of beliefs on our body. What you continually *give* to your body with your beliefs or strong feelings, you must *receive* in your body.

Every feeling you have saturates every cell and organ in your entire body. When you have good feelings, you are giving love and you receive the full force of health through your body at an astounding rate. When you have bad feelings, the tension causes your nerves and cells to contract, the vital chemical production in your body changes, your blood vessels contract, and your breathing becomes shallow, all of which reduces the force of health in your organs and your entire body. Disease is simply the result of a body's not being at ease over a long period of time, because of negative feelings like stress, worry, and fear.

> *"Your emotions affect every cell in your body. Mind and body, mental and physical, are intertwined."*

Thomas Tutko (B. 1931)
SPORTS PSYCHOLOGIST AND AUTHOR

The World Inside Your Body

There is an entire world inside you! To realize the power you have over your body, you need to know about this world – because all of it is under your command!

All the cells in your body have a role to play, and they work together for the sole purpose of giving you life. Some cells are the leaders of particular regions or organs, and they manage and direct all the working cells in their region, like your heart, brain, liver, kidneys, and lungs. The leader cell of an organ directs and manages all the other cells working in that organ, ensuring order and harmony so the organ works perfectly. Patrol cells travel throughout the sixty thousand miles of blood vessels in your body to maintain order and peace. When there is a disturbance, such as a scratch to the skin, the patrol cells immediately signal the alert, and the appropriate repair team rushes to the area. For a scratch, the first on the scene is the blood-clotting team, and they work to arrest the blood flow. After their work is done, the tissue and skin teams move in to do the repair work to the area, mending the tissue, and sealing the skin.

If an intruder enters your body, like a bacterial infection or virus, the memory cells immediately take an imprint (snapshot) of the intruder. The imprint is checked against their records to see if there is a match with previous intruders. If they find a match, the memory cells immediately notify the relevant attack team to destroy the intruder. If there is no match, the memory cells open up a new file on the intruder, and *all* the attack teams are summoned to move in and destroy the intruder. Whichever attack team is successful in destroying the intruder is then recorded by the memory cells in their files. If the intruder returns, the memory cells will know who they are dealing with and exactly how to deal with them.

If for any reason a cell of your body begins to change its behavior and cease to work for the good of the body, the patrol cells signal the rescue team to rush in to repair the cell. If a cell needs a particular chemical to be repaired, it is found inside your natural pharmacy. You have a complete pharmacy operating inside you that can produce every healing chemical that a pharmaceutical company can produce.

All cells must work as a team, 24 hours a day, 7 days a week, for their entire life. Their sole purpose is to maintain the life and health in your body. You have around 100 trillion cells in your body. That's 100,000,000,000,000 cells who are working nonstop to give you life! All 100 trillion cells are under your command, and you are commanding them and instructing them with your thoughts, feelings, and beliefs.

Whatever you believe about your body, your cells believe too. They don't question anything you think, feel, or believe. In fact, they hear every thought, feeling, and belief you have.

If you think or say, "I always get jetlag when I travel," your cells receive "jetlag" as a command, and they must carry out your instructions. Think and feel that you have a weight problem, and your cells receive the order of a weight problem. They must follow your instructions and keep your body in an overweight condition. Be afraid you might catch an illness, and your cells receive the message of the illness, and they immediately get busy creating the symptoms of the illness. Your cells' responding to your every command is simply the law of attraction working inside your body.

"Face towards the perfect image of every organ, and the shadows of disease will never touch you."

Robert Collier (1885-1950)
NEW THOUGHT AUTHOR

What do you want? What would you love? Because that is what you must give to your body. Your cells are your most loyal subjects who serve you without question, and so whatever you think, whatever you feel, becomes the law of your body. If you want to feel as good as you did when you were a child, then give your cells those commands: "I feel amazing today." "I have so much energy." "I have perfect eyesight." "I can eat whatever I want and maintain my ideal weight." "I sleep like a baby every night." You are the ruler of a kingdom, and whatever you think and feel becomes the law of your kingdom – the law within your body.

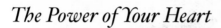

The Power of Your Heart

> *"In some sense man is a microcosm of the universe;
> therefore what man is, is a clue to the universe."*
>
> *David Bohm* (1917-1992)
>
> QUANTUM PHYSICIST

The inside of your body is an exact map of our solar
system and the universe. Your heart is the sun and the center
of your body system. Your organs are the planets, and just
as the planets depend on the sun to remain in balance and
harmony, so do all the organs in your body depend on your
heart to remain in balance and harmony.

Scientists at the Institute of HeartMath in California have
shown that feeling love, gratitude, and appreciation in your
heart boosts your immune system; increases vital chemical
production; increases physical vitality and vigor; reduces
stress hormone levels, high blood pressure, anxiety, guilt, and
burnout; and improves glucose regulation in diabetics. Feelings
of love also create a higher degree of harmony in the rhythm
of your heart. HeartMath has shown that the magnetic field
of the heart is 5,000 times more powerful than the magnetic
field of the brain, and reaches out several feet from our body.

Other scientists are revolutionizing our understanding
of the affect of love on our health, through experiments with
water. What does water have to do with health? Your body

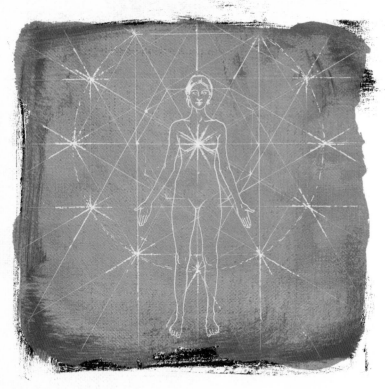

is made up of 70 percent water! The inside of your head is 80 percent water!

Researchers in Japan, Russia, Europe, and the United States have discovered that when water is exposed to positive words and feelings such as love and gratitude, the energy level of the water not only increases, but the structure of the water changes, making it perfectly harmonious. The higher the positive feeling, the more beautiful and harmonious the water becomes. When water is exposed to negative emotions, such as hate, the energy level of the water decreases, and chaotic changes occur, negatively affecting the structure of the water.

If human emotions can change the structure of water, can you imagine what your feelings are doing to the health of your body? Your cells are made of mostly water! The center of every cell is water, and each cell is completely surrounded by a layer of water.

Can you imagine the impact of love and gratitude on your body? Can you imagine the power of love and gratitude to restore health? When you feel love, your love affects the water of the 100 trillion cells in your body!

How to Use the Power of Love for Perfect Health

"Where there is the greatest love, there are always miracles."

Willa Cather (1873-1947)
PULITZER PRIZE–WINNING NOVELIST

To receive the health you want and love, you must give love! In the face of any sickness, give good feelings about health, because only love brings perfect health. You cannot give bad feelings about sickness and receive health. If you hate or fear a disease, you will be giving out bad feelings, and disease can never go away through bad feelings. When you give thoughts and feelings of what you want, your cells receive the full force of health. When you give negative thoughts and feelings of what you don't want, the force of health to your cells reduces! It doesn't matter if you feel bad about a subject that has nothing to do with your health; when you feel bad, you reduce the force of health to your body. But when you feel love for anything – for a sunny day, new house, friend, or promotion – your body receives the full force of health.

Gratitude is the great multiplier, so say *thank you* for your health every single day. All the money in the world cannot buy health, because it is a gift from life, and so more than anything else, be grateful for your health! It's the best health insurance you can ever take, because gratitude is the assurance of health!

Be grateful for your body instead of finding fault with it. Every time you have a thought of something you don't like about your body, remember that the water inside your body is receiving your feelings. Instead say *thank you* with all your heart for what you do like about your body, and ignore the things you don't like.

"Love draws forth love."

Saint Teresa of Ávila (1515-1582)

NUN, MYSTIC, AND WRITER

Before you eat food or drink water, look at what you're about to eat or drink and feel love and gratitude. Make sure your conversations are positive when you are sitting down to a meal.

Blessing food gives love and gratitude for food. As you bless food, you change the structure of the water in the food and its effect on your body. Blessing water with love and gratitude does the same thing. Your positive feelings of love can change the structure of water in everything – so use the power.

You can give love and gratitude and use their power while receiving any medical treatment. If you can imagine being well, you can *feel* being well, and if you can feel it, you can receive it. To see your health improve, all you have to do is give love more than 50 percent of the time. Just 51 percent is the tipping point from sickness to health.

When having your eyesight checked or blood pressure checked, or if you're having a general checkup, receiving results from tests, or anything concerning your health, it is very important that you are feeling good during it and while receiving the results, in order to receive a good outcome. By the law of attraction, the outcome of the checkup or tests must match the frequency you're on, so to bring the good outcome you want, you must be on the frequency to receive it! Life does not happen the other way around. The outcome of every situation in your life will always match your frequency

because that is the law of attraction! To get yourself onto a
good feeling frequency about a test, imagine the outcome you
want and feel that you have already received that outcome.
Every possible outcome can happen, but you must be on
a good feeling frequency to receive good outcomes.

"Possibilities and miracles mean the same thing."

Prentice Mulford (1834-1891)
NEW THOUGHT AUTHOR

Imagine and feel having the health you want in your body.
If you want to restore your eyesight, give love for perfect
vision and imagine having it. Give love for perfect hearing and
imagine having it. Give love for the perfect weight, perfect
body, perfect health of an organ, and imagine having it, and
be utterly grateful for everything you do have! Your body will
change into whatever you want, but it can only do it through
feelings of love and gratitude.

When a young, fit woman was told she had a rare heart
disease, her life crumbled around her. She suddenly felt
weak and fragile. Her future – a normal, healthy life – had
disappeared with the prognosis. She was terrified of leaving
her two young daughters motherless. But this woman decided
she was going to do everything she could to heal her heart.

She refused to entertain any negative thoughts about her
heart. She placed her right hand on her heart every day and

imagined her strong, healthy heart. Every morning when she woke, she gave the deepest thanks for her strong, healthy heart. She imagined the cardiologists telling her that she was cured. She did these things every day for four months, and when her cardiologists checked her heart four months later, they were dumbfounded. They checked and rechecked the old tests against the new test, because the new test showed that the woman's heart was perfectly strong and healthy.

This woman lived according to love's law of attraction. She did not own the prognosis of a diseased heart in her mind, but she gave love for a healthy heart, and she owned a healthy heart instead. If you are facing any kind of illness, do your best not to own it with your thoughts and words. Don't hate an illness either, because that is giving negativity to it. Instead, give love to health, own health, and make it yours.

> *"Keep your mind as much as you can from dwelling on your ailment. Think of strength and power and you will draw it to you. Think of health and you get it."*

> Prentice Mulford (1834–1891)
> NEW THOUGHT AUTHOR

Every moment you feel love for your health, the force of love is eliminating any negativity in your body! If you find it difficult to feel good about your health, all that matters is that you feel love for anything, so surround yourself with everything you love, and use those things to feel as good as you can. Use everything you can in the outside world so that you feel love. Watch movies that make you laugh and feel good, not movies that make you feel tense or sad. Listen to music that makes you feel good. Get people to tell you jokes that make you laugh, or have them tell you funny stories about their most embarrassing moments. You know the things you love. You know your favorite things. You know what makes you happy, so draw on them all and feel as good as you can. Use the Creation Process. Use the Keys to Power. Remember it only takes giving love and good feelings a minimum of 51 percent of the time to reach the tipping point and change everything!

If you want to help somebody who is ill, you can use the Creation Process and imagine and feel full health being restored to them. Although you cannot override what another person is giving to the law of attraction, your power can help them rise to a frequency where they can receive health.

Beauty Comes from Love

"As love grows in you, beauty grows too. For love is the beauty of the soul."

Saint Augustine of Hippo (354-430)
THEOLOGIAN AND BISHOP

All beauty comes from the force of love. Unlimited beauty is available to you through love, but the problem is that most people find fault and criticize their body more than they appreciate it. Looking at your faults and being unhappy about anything about your body does not bring beauty to you! All it brings is more faults and more unhappiness.

The beauty business is enormous, yet unlimited beauty is being poured down to you in every second. But you have to give love to receive it! The happier you are, the more beautiful you will be. Lines will fade, skin will tighten and begin to glow, hair will become thicker and stronger, eyes will begin to sparkle, and their color will intensify. And more than anything else, you will see the proof that beauty comes from love when people are drawn to you wherever you go.

You Really Are as Old as You Feel

Ancient texts say that people once lived for hundreds and hundreds of years. Some lived for eight hundred years, some lived for five or six hundred years, but longevity was commonplace. So what's happened? People changed what they believed. Instead of believing in living for hundreds and hundreds of years, people changed their beliefs over generations, and they came to believe in a reduced life expectancy.

We have inherited those beliefs of a reduced life expectancy. From the time we are born, the belief of how long we can live has been sewn into the fabric of our minds and our hearts. And from there we literally program our bodies from an early age to live for a certain amount of time, and our bodies age according to how we program them.

"There is nothing in biology yet found that indicates the inevitability of death. This suggests to me that it is not at all inevitable and that it is only a matter of time before biologists discover what it is that is causing us the trouble."

Richard Feynman (1918-1988)
NOBEL PRIZE–WINNING QUANTUM PHYSICIST

If you possibly can, don't put a ceiling on how long you can live. All it will take is one person to break the limits of life expectancy, and that person will change the course of life expectancy for all humanity. One person after another will follow, because when one person lives far beyond the current life expectancy, other people will believe and feel they can do it too, and they will!

When you believe and feel that aging and deterioration are inevitable, then they will happen. Your cells, your organs, and your body receive your beliefs and feelings. *Feel* young and stop feeling your age. Feeling your age is just a belief you've been given and a program you've given to your body. You can change the command you're giving whenever you want, by changing what you believe!

How do you change your beliefs? By giving love! Negative beliefs, such as beliefs of limitation, aging, or disease, do not come from love. When you give love, when you feel good, love melts away any negativity, including negative beliefs that harm you.

> *"The love that gushes for all is the real elixir of life — the fountain of bodily longevity. It is the lack of this that always produces the feeling of age."*
>
> *Josiah Gilbert Holland* (1819-1881)
>
> AUTHOR

Love Is Truth

When you were a little child, you were flexible and fluid because you had not formed or accepted as many negative beliefs about life. As you got older, you took on more feelings of limitation and negativity, which caused you to become more set in your ways and less flexible. This is not an amazing life; this is a limited life.

The more you love, the more the force of love will melt away negativity in your body and in your mind. And you can feel love melting away everything negative when you're happy, grateful, and joyful. You can feel it! You feel light, you feel invincible, and you feel on top of the world.

As you give more and more love, you will notice changes start to happen to your body. Food will taste better, colors will get brighter, sounds will become clearer, moles or little marks on your body will begin to fade and disappear. Your body will begin to feel more flexible; stiffness and little creaks will begin to vanish. When you give love and experience the miracles in your body, you will be left in no doubt that love is the source of health!

Love Is Behind Every Miracle

All miracles are the force of love at work. Miracles are created by turning away from negativity and focusing on only love. Even if you have been a pessimist all your life, it is never too late.

A pessimist is exactly how one man described himself. When this man received the surprise news from his wife that they were expecting their third child, his every thought was of how negative the impact of a third child would be in their lives. But what he didn't realize was exactly how those negative thoughts and feelings would play out for him.

At just over the halfway point of his wife's pregnancy, she had to be rushed to the hospital and an emergency C-section had to be performed to deliver their baby. Three separate specialists said that at 23 weeks' gestation, the baby had a zero percent chance of survival. The man was brought to his knees. He had never expected to lose a child.

After the C-section, the father was taken to the side of the room to see his son, the smallest baby he had ever seen. His son was born 10 inches in length and weighed only 12 ounces. The medical staff tried to inflate the baby's lungs with a ventilator, but his heart rate was decreasing. The specialist said there was nothing they would be able to do. The father screamed out in his mind, "Please!" At that exact moment, the ventilator inflated his son's lungs and his heart rate began to climb.

Days passed. All the physicians in the hospital kept saying that the baby would not make it. But this man who had been a pessimist all of his life began to imagine what he wanted. Every night when he went to bed, he imagined the light of love shining on his son. When he woke in the morning, he would give thanks to God that his son had survived through the night.

Each day his son made progress, and he overcame every obstacle that was thrown at him. After four grueling months in intensive care, he and his wife were able to take their baby – who had been given a *zero percent chance* of survival – home.

Love is behind every miracle.

POINTS OF POWER

- *What you continually give to your body with your beliefs or strong feelings, you receive in your body. Every feeling you have saturates every cell and organ in your entire body.*

- *You are the ruler of a kingdom, and your cells are your most loyal subjects who serve you without question, so whatever you think and feel becomes the law of your kingdom – the law within your body.*

- *When you give negative thoughts and feelings of what you don't want, the force of health to your cells reduces! When you feel love for anything – for a sunny day, new house, friend, or promotion – your body receives the full force of health.*

- *Gratitude is the great multiplier, so say thank you for your health every single day.*

- *Say thank you with all your heart for what you do like about your body, and ignore the things you don't like.*

- *To see your health improve, give love to health more than fifty percent of the time. Just 51 percent is the tipping point from sickness to health.*

- *If you are facing illness, do your best not to own it with your thoughts and words. Instead, give love to health, own health, and make it yours.*

- *Give love for the perfect weight, perfect body, perfect health of an organ, and imagine having it, and be utterly grateful for everything you do have!*

- *If you believe that your body will deteriorate with age, you are giving out that belief, and the law of attraction must return those circumstances to you.*

- *Feel young and stop feeling your age.*

- *Your body will change into whatever you want, through your feelings of love and gratitude.*

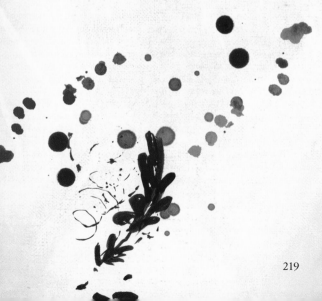

THE POWER
AND YOU

*"The power for happiness, for good, for everything
we need of life is within each one of us. The power
is there – unlimited power."*

Robert Collier (1885-1950)

NEW THOUGHT AUTHOR

Everything has a frequency – everything! Every word has
a frequency, every sound, every color, every tree, animal, plant,
mineral, every material object. Every type of food and liquid
has a frequency. Every place, city, and country has a frequency.
The elements of air, fire, earth, and water all have frequencies.
Health, disease, plenty of money, a lack of money, success
and failure all have frequencies. Every event, situation, and
circumstance has a frequency. Even your name has a frequency.
But the real name of your frequency is what you are feeling!
And whatever you're feeling is bringing *everything* into your
life that's on a similar frequency to you.

When you are feeling happy, and you keep feeling
happy, then only happy people, circumstances, and events
can come into your life. If you feel stressed, and you keep
feeling stressed, then only more stress can come into your life

221

through people, circumstances, and events. You have seen this happen when you've been rushing because you're running late. Rushing is a negative feeling, and as surely as the sun shines, when you rush and feel the fear of being late, you bring every delay and obstacle into your path. It's the law of attraction working in your life.

Do you see how important it is that you feel good before you begin your day? If you don't take the time to feel good, then you can't receive good things in your day. And once negative things come, it takes far more effort to change them, because once they're in front of you, you really believe in them! It is much easier to take the time to feel good so that they don't come in the first place. You can change anything in your life by changing the way you feel, but isn't it a better idea to have more good things come to you in the first place?

Watch the Movie of Your Life!

Life is magical! What happens in one day of your life is more magical than any fantasy movie you can see, but you have to *look* at what is happening with the same concentration as when you watch a movie. If you're watching a movie and you get distracted with a phone call or you fall asleep, you miss what happens. It's the same thing with the movie of your life that is constantly showing on the screen of your day. If you are walking around asleep and you're not alert, you miss the messages and synchronicities that are constantly speaking to you, guiding and directing you in your life!

Life is responding to you. Life is communicating with you. There are no accidents or coincidences: every single thing has a frequency, and when anything comes into your life, it means it's on the same frequency as you are. Everything you see – every sign, color, person, object – everything you hear, every circumstance and event is on your frequency.

> *"So astounding are the facts in this connection that it would seem as though the Creator himself had electrically designed this planet."*

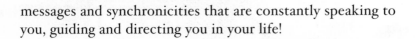

Nikola Tesla (1856-1943)
INVENTOR OF THE RADIO AND ALTERNATING CURRENT

You know that when you're driving and you see a police car, you suddenly become more alert. There is a reason that you saw the police car and most likely it is telling you, "Be more alert!" Seeing the police car may mean even more to you, but you have to ask the question "What is this telling me?" to receive the answer. Police represent law and order, so the police car may be a message of something that's out of order in your life, such as you forgot to call your friend back, or you didn't thank someone for something.

When you hear an ambulance siren, what is it saying to you? Is it telling you to be grateful for your health? Is it reminding you to give love and thanks for the health of the people in your life? When you see a fire engine race past you with its lights and sirens going, what is it telling *you*? Is it saying there's a fire somewhere in your life that you need to put out? Or is it telling you to fire up your love? Only you will know the meaning of the things that come into your life, but you must be alert to what is happening around you so you can ask questions and receive the meaning of the message for you.

You are being given messages and feedback constantly, and you have been receiving these messages *all* your life! Whenever I hear something, even if they are words from a conversation of two strangers who are standing near me, if I can hear their words, their words have meaning in my life. Their words are a message for me, they're relevant to me, and they're giving me feedback on my life. If I am traveling and I notice a sign and I read the words, those words have meaning for me, they're a message for me, and they're relevant to me. They're relevant to me because I am on the same frequency as they are. If I were on a different frequency, I wouldn't notice the sign, and I wouldn't be in earshot of a conversation.

Every single thing that surrounds me in my day is speaking to me, giving me constant feedback and messages. If I notice that the people around me aren't as happy or smiling as much as they were, I know my feeling frequency has dropped, and immediately I think of things I love, one after the other, until I feel happier.

"We need to be the change we wish to see in the world."

Mahatma Gandhi (1869-1948)
INDIAN POLITICAL LEADER

Your Secret Symbol

You can play with the law of attraction by asking to see physical evidence of the force of love. Think of something you love, and make it your symbol of the force of love. Whenever you see your symbol or hear it, you will know that the force of love is with you. I use illuminating, sparkling light as my symbol, so if the sun hits my eyes, or its light reflects off something into my eyes, or if I see anything that reflects light and sparkles, I know it is the force of love and it is with me. When I am overflowing with joy and filled with love, light reflects off everything around me. My sister uses rainbows as her symbol, and when she is overflowing with love and gratitude, wherever she looks there are rainbows of light and all kinds of rainbows all around her. You can use stars, gold, silver, or any color, animal, bird, tree, or flower that you love as your symbol. You can choose words or sounds as your secret symbol. Just make sure that whatever you choose, you choose something you absolutely love and adore.

If you want, you can also choose a symbol as a warning sign from the force of love to you, telling you to pay attention.

In truth you are receiving messages and warnings all the time. When you drop something, when you trip, catch your clothes on something, or when you bump into something – they're all warnings and messages you're receiving to stop what you're thinking or feeling! There are no accidents or coincidences in life – everything is synchronicity – because everything has a frequency. It's simply the physics of life and the universe in action.

> *"When I look at the solar system, I see the earth at the right distance from the sun to receive the proper amounts of heat and light. This did not happen by chance."*
>
> *Isaac Newton* (1643-1727)
> MATHEMATICIAN AND PHYSICIST

Life Is Magical

Love and I have a thing going on, and it is the most magical and exciting relationship anyone can ever have. I want to share with you how I live each day with this knowledge.

When I wake each morning, I am grateful to be alive and for everyone and everything in my life. I spend fifteen minutes every morning feeling love and sending it out to the world.

I imagine my day. I imagine and feel love for my day going well. I imagine and feel love for each thing in my day going well, before I do it. I place the force of love ahead of me in everything I do, by feeling love inside me as much as I can *before* I do anything! I don't open emails or packages, make or take important phone calls, or do anything important unless I am feeling good.

When I get dressed in the morning I feel enormous gratitude for my clothes. To save time, I also ask the question "What is the perfect outfit to wear today?" A few years ago I decided to play with the law of attraction and my wardrobe. Instead of trying to work out whether this skirt will go with that top, and sometimes putting things on and taking them off again because they didn't work together (which attracts more things not working), I decided to hand my styling over to the force of love. So all I did was *imagine* what it would *feel* like if everything I put on looked great. After imagining it, feeling it, and asking the question "What will I wear today?" I now stand in awe at how good my clothes look and feel when I get dressed.

I stay aware when walking down the street and notice the people passing me. I send thoughts and feelings of love to as many people as I can. I look at each person's face, feel love inside me, and imagine them receiving it. I know the force of love is the source of abundance of money, happy relationships, great health, and anything anyone loves, so I send people love,

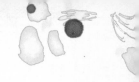

because I know in doing that, I am sending them whatever they need.

When I see a person who seems to have a particular need, someone who can't afford to buy something they want, for instance, I send them thoughts of abundance of money. If a person seems upset, I send them happiness. If someone seems stressed and they're rushing, I send them thoughts of peace and joy. Whether I am shopping for groceries, walking down the street, or driving, whenever I am among people, I do my best to send love as much as possible. I know too that whenever I see anyone with a particular need, it's also a message for me to be grateful for money, happiness, and the peace and joy in my life.

When I am in a plane, I send love to everyone. When I am in a restaurant, I send love to the people and to the food. In dealing with organizations or companies, or when I am shopping in stores, I send love to them all.

When I get in my car to drive somewhere, I imagine arriving back home happy and well, and I say, "Thank you." When I am about to drive, I ask, "What is the best road to take?" Each time I walk into and out of my house, I say "Thank you" for my home. When I am shopping at the supermarket, I ask, "What else do I need?" and "Do I have everything?" I always receive the answers.

*"Certainly, knowledge is a lock and its key
is the question."*

Ja'far al-Sadiq (702-765)
ISLAMIC SPIRITUAL LEADER

Every day I ask many questions, sometimes hundreds
of questions. I ask, "How am I doing today?" "What should
I do in this situation?" "What is the best decision?" "What
is the solution to this problem?" "Which choice is the best
choice for me to make?" "Is this person or company right?"
"How can I feel better?" "How can I lift my feelings higher?"
"Where do I need to give love today?" "What can I see that
I'm grateful for?"

When you ask a question, you are *giving* a question,
and you must *receive* the answer! But you have to be alert
and aware to see or hear the answers to your questions. You
may receive the answer through reading something, hearing
something, or dreaming something. Sometimes suddenly you
will just know the answer to your question. But you will always
receive the answer!

If I have misplaced something, like my keys, I ask, "Where
are my keys?" I always receive the answer. But it doesn't stop
there. When I find my keys I ask, "What is this telling me?"
In other words, why did I misplace my keys? Because there is a
reason for everything! There are no accidents or coincidences.
Sometimes the answer I receive is "Slow down, you are

rushing." Sometimes the answer is "Your wallet is not in your handbag" and I look around in the room where I found my keys and there is my wallet. Sometimes I don't receive an answer right away, but as I'm walking out the door, the phone rings and the appointment I was going to has been canceled. Immediately I know that misplacing my keys was happening for a positive reason. I love the way life works, but you can't receive any answers or feedback unless you ask questions!

Sometimes life may throw some tricky thing my way, but I know when it happens that I attracted it to me. I always ask how I attracted any problem so I can learn from it – and so I won't do it again!

In return for everything I receive, I give my love to the world as much as I can. I look for the good in everything and in everyone. I am grateful for everything. And as I give love, I feel the force of love sweeping through me, filling me with such love and joy that it takes my breath away. Even when you try to give love back for everything you've received, the force of love multiplies that love and returns even *more* love to you! When you feel this happen just once in your life, you will never be the same again.

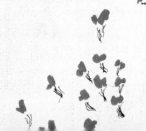

Love Will Do Anything for You

You can harness the force of love to help you with anything in your life. You can hand over anything you need to remember, and ask the force of love to remind you of it at the perfect time. You can have the force of love be your alarm clock and wake you at the time you want. The force of love will be your personal assistant, money manager, personal health trainer, relationship counselor, and it will manage your money, your weight, your food, your relationships, or any task you want to give it. But it will only do these things for you when you unite with it through love, appreciation, and gratitude! It will only do these things for you when you join forces with it through love and let go of your white-knuckle grip on life in trying to control everything on your own.

> *"As your faith is strengthened you will find that there is no longer the need to have a sense of control, that things will flow as they will, and that you will flow with them, to your great delight and benefit."*
>
> *Wingate Paine* (1915-1987)
> AUTHOR AND PHOTOGRAPHER

Unite forces with the greatest force in life. And whatever you want the force of love to do for you, imagine having it, feel having it with absolute love and gratitude, and you will receive it.

Use your imagination and think of all the things the force of love can do for you. The force of love is *the* intelligence of life and the universe. If you can imagine the intelligence that can create a flower or a cell in a human body, then you will appreciate that there isn't a single question you can ask that you won't receive the perfect answer for whatever your situation. Love will do anything for you, but you have to unite with it, through love, to realize its power in your life.

What Difference Does It Make?

> *"Out of clutter, find simplicity. From discord,*
> *find harmony. In the middle of difficulty*
> *lies opportunity."*

Albert Einstein (1879-1955)

NOBEL PRIZE—WINNING PHYSICIST

If your mind is consumed with too many details, the little details will distract you and pull you down. You can't be single-minded about feeling good if you're chasing your tail over small details that don't matter. What difference does it make if you get your clothes into the dry cleaners before they close, really? What difference does it make to *your* life if your sports team didn't win this week? There's always next week. What difference does it make if you missed the bus? What difference does it make if the grocery store has run out of oranges? What difference does it make if you have to stand in a line for a few minutes? In the whole scheme of things, what difference do those little things make?

Small details distract you, and they can sabotage your life. If you give too much importance to unnecessary details, you will not feel good. None of those things matters in the scheme of your life! Not one of them! Simplify your life. Do it to protect your good feelings. Do it, because when you get rid of the small details, you create space for everything you want to pour into your life.

You Give Life Meaning

You give the meaning to everything in life. No situation comes with a label of good or bad. Everything is neutral. A rainbow and a thunderstorm are not good or bad, they're just a rainbow and a thunderstorm. You give the meaning to a rainbow by how you feel about it. You give the meaning to a thunderstorm by how you feel about it. You give the meaning to everything by the way you feel. A job is not good or bad, it's just a job, but how you feel about your job determines whether it will be good or bad for you. A relationship is not good or bad in and of itself, it's just a relationship, but how you feel about a relationship determines whether it will be good or bad for you.

> *"Nothing is either good or bad, but thinking makes it so."*
>
> *William Shakespeare* (1564-1616)
> ENGLISH PLAYWRIGHT

If someone harms another person, the law of attraction responds unfailingly. It may use police or laws or any number of ways to give back to the person exactly what they gave, but one thing is certain with the law of attraction; we receive back what we give. If you hear of someone being harmed by another person, feel compassion for the person harmed, but don't judge anyone. If you judge someone and think they are bad, you are not giving love. And in thinking that someone else is bad, you have in effect labeled yourself as bad. Whatever you give, *you* receive. When you give out bad feelings about someone else, no matter what they have done, those bad feelings come back to *you*! They come back to you with the same force you sent out, creating negative circumstances in *your* life. There are *no* excuses for the force of love!

> *"The life that goes out in love to all life is the life that is full, and rich, and continually expanding in beauty and in power."*
>
> *Ralph Waldo Trine* (1866-1958)
> NEW THOUGHT AUTHOR

Love Is the Power to the World

The force of love has no opposite. There is no other power in life but love. There isn't a force of negativity. In ancient times, negativity was sometimes described as "the devil" or "evil." Being tempted by evil or the devil simply meant being tempted to fall into negative thoughts and feelings, rather than standing firm in the positive force of love. There is no force of negativity. There is only one force, and that force is love.

All the negative things you see in the world are always, always manifestations of a lack of love. Whether that negativity is in a person, place, circumstance, or event, it has

always come from a lack of love. There isn't a force of sadness; sadness is a lack of happiness, and all happiness comes from love. There isn't a force of failure; failure is a lack of success, and all success comes from love. There isn't a force of illness; illness is a lack of health, and all health comes from love. There isn't a force of poverty; poverty is a lack of abundance, and all abundance comes from love. Love is the positive force of life, and *any* negative condition *always* comes from a lack of love.

When people reach the tipping point of giving more love than negativity, we will see negativity vanish from the planet at a rapid rate. Imagine it! Every single time you choose to give love, your love is helping to tip the entire world into positivity! Some people believe that we are very close to the tipping point now. Whether they're right or not, more than ever, *now* is the time to give love and positivity. Do it for your life. Do it for your country. Do it for the world.

> *"When the heart is set right, then the personal life is cultivated. When the personal life is cultivated, then the home life is regulated. When the home life is regulated, then the national life is orderly: And when the national life is orderly, then the world is at peace."*

Confucius (551-479 BC)
CHINESE PHILOSOPHER

You have so much power in the world because you have so much love you can give.

POINTS OF POWER

- *Everything has a frequency – everything! And whatever you're feeling is bringing everything into your life that's on a similar frequency to you.*

- *Life is responding to you. Life is communicating with you. Everything you see – every sign, color, person, object – everything you hear, every circumstance and event, are on your frequency.*

- *When you are feeling happy, and you keep feeling happy, then only happy people, circumstances, and events can come into your life.*

- *There are no accidents or coincidences in life – everything is synchronicity – because everything has a frequency. It's simply the physics of life and the universe in action.*

- *Think of something you love, and make it your symbol of the force of love. Whenever you see your symbol or hear it, you will know that the force of love is with you.*

- *Place the force of love ahead of you in everything you do. Imagine each thing in your day going well, and feel love inside yourself as much as you can, before you do anything.*

- *Ask questions every day. When you ask a question you are giving a question, and you must receive the answer!*

- *Harness the force of love to help you with anything in your life. The force of love will be your personal assistant, money manager, personal health trainer, and relationship counselor.*

- *If your mind is consumed with too many details, the details will distract you and pull you down. Simplify your life, and don't give too much importance to the little things. What difference does it make?*

- *The force of love has no opposite. There is no other power in life but love. All the negative things you see in the world are always, always a lack of love.*

THE POWER
AND LIFE

A human being cannot imagine *not* existing. We can imagine our body not being alive, but we simply cannot imagine not existing. Why do you think that is? Do you think it's a fluke of nature? It's not. You cannot imagine yourself not existing because it's impossible for you not to exist! If you could imagine it, you could create it, and you can never create it! You have always existed and you will always exist because you are a part of creation.

"There has never been a time when you and I and the kings gathered here have not existed, nor will there be a time when we will cease to exist. As the same person inhabits the body through childhood, youth, and old age, so too at the time of death, he attains another body. The wise are not deluded by these changes."

Bhagavad Gita (5TH CENTURY BC)

ANCIENT HINDU TEXT

So what happens when a person dies? The body doesn't go into nonexistence, because there's no such thing. It integrates itself into the elements. And the being that is inside you – the *real* you – doesn't go into nonexistence either. The very word "being" tells you that you will always be! You are not a human "been"! You are an eternal being living temporarily in a human body. If you stopped existing, there would be an empty space in the universe, and the whole universe would collapse into that empty space.

The only reason you can't see another being after they have left their body is that you can't see the frequency of love. You can't see the frequency of ultraviolet light either, and the frequency of love, which is the frequency they're on, is the highest frequency in creation. The greatest scientific equipment in the world cannot even come close to detecting the frequency of love. But remember that you can *feel* love, so if there is someone you can't see anymore, you can feel them on the frequency of love. You can't feel them in grief or despair because those frequencies are nowhere near the frequency they're on. But when you are on the highest frequencies of love and gratitude, you can feel them. They are never far away from you and you are never separated from them. You are always connected to *everything* in life through the force of love.

Heaven Is Within You

"All the principles of heaven and earth are living inside you."

Morihei Ueshiba (1883-1969)

FOUNDER OF THE MARTIAL ARTS AIKIDO

Ancient texts say that "heaven is within you," and what they're talking about is the frequency of your being. When you leave your human body, you are automatically on the highest frequency of pure love, because that's the frequency of your being. In ancient times this highest frequency of pure love was called heaven.

But heaven is for you to find here in this lifetime – not when your body dies. You are to find heaven here, while you're on Earth. And indeed heaven is within you, because heaven is the frequency of your being. To find heaven on Earth is to live your life at the same frequency as your being – pure love and joy.

For the Love of Life

> *"The question is not really whether or not you go on,*
> *but rather how are you going to enjoy it?"*

Robert Thurman (B. 1941)

BUDDHIST WRITER AND ACADEMIC

You are an eternal being. You have all the time in the world to experience everything. There's no lack of time because you have forever! You have so many adventures ahead, so many things to experience. Not just adventures on Earth, because once we've mastered Earth, we will begin new adventures in other worlds. There are galaxies, dimensions, and life that we can't even imagine now, but we will experience all of them. And we will experience them together because *we* are a part of creation. Billions of years from now, when we look out into creation for our next adventure, there will be worlds among worlds, galaxies among galaxies, and unlimited dimensions, stretching out before us for all eternity.

And so do you think with all this that perhaps you are a wee bit more special than you ever considered yourself to be? Do you think perhaps you might be a little more valuable than you thought? You, every person you know, and every person who has ever lived have no end!

Don't you just want to wrap your arms around life and say *thank you*? Aren't you excited for the adventures ahead?

Don't you want to stand on a mountaintop and cry out with joy *Yes!* to a never-ending life?

The Purpose of Your Life

> *"You have no cause for anything but gratitude and joy."*
>
> *Gautama Buddha* (563-483 BC)
> FOUNDER OF BUDDHISM

The purpose of your life is joy, and so what do you think is the greatest joy in life? Giving! If a person had told me six years ago that the greatest joy in life is giving, I would have said, "That's fine for you to say. I am struggling to survive and can barely make ends meet, and so I have nothing to give."

The greatest joy in life is giving because unless you give, you will always be struggling to survive. Life will be full of one problem after another, and just when you think everything is going along fine, something else will happen to throw you back into struggle and difficulty. The greatest joy in life is giving, and there is only one thing you can give – your love! Your love, your joy, your positivity, your excitement, your gratitude, and your passion are the true and everlasting things in life. All the riches in the world cannot even come close to the most priceless gift in all of creation – the love inside you!

Give the best of you. Give your love because it is the magnet to *all* the riches of life. And your life will become richer than you thought was possible, because when you give love, you are fulfilling the entire purpose of your life. When you give love, you will receive back so much love and joy that you will feel it is almost more than you can take. But you *can* take unlimited love and joy, because it's who you are.

> *"Someday when men have conquered the winds, the waves, the tides and gravity, we will harness for God the energies of love, and then, for a second time in the history of the world, man will have discovered fire."*
>
> *Pierre Teilhard de Chardin* (1881-1955)
>
> PRIEST AND PHILOSOPHER

You came into this world with your love, and it is the only thing you take with you. While you are here, every time you choose the positive, every time you choose to feel good, you are giving your love, and with it you light up the world. And everything you can wish for, everything you can dream of, everything you love will follow you wherever you go.

You have the greatest force in the universe within you. And with it, you *will* have an amazing life!

The Power is within you.

The Beginning

POINTS OF POWER

- *You have always existed and you will always exist because you are a part of creation.*

- *You, every person you know, and every person who has ever lived has no end!*

- *To find heaven on Earth is to live your life at the same frequency as your being – pure love and joy.*

- *The greatest joy in life is giving, because unless you give, you will always be struggling to survive.*

- *Your love, your joy, your positivity, your excitement, your gratitude, and your passion are the true and everlasting things in life. All the riches in the world cannot even come close to the most priceless gift in all of creation – the love inside you!*

- *Give your love because it is the magnet to all the riches of life.*

- *While you are here, every time you choose the positive, every time you choose to feel good, you are giving your love, and with it you light up the world.*

*May The Power bring you love and joy
for your entire existence.*

*That is my intention for you,
and for the world.*

About the Author

Rhonda Byrne's intention is: *joy to billions*.

She began her journey with *The Secret* film,
viewed by millions across the planet. She
followed with *The Secret* book, a worldwide
bestseller now available in 46 languages.

Now with *The Power*, Rhonda Byrne continues
her groundbreaking work, as she reveals the
single greatest force in our universe.

TS0222PWB_US12FA